Early years activities

PHOTOCOPIABLES

WRITING HOMEWORK

**Published by Scholastic Ltd,
Villiers House,
Clarendon Avenue,
Leamington Spa,
Warwickshire CV32 5PR**

© 1997 Scholastic Ltd
1 2 3 4 5 6 7 8 9   7 8 9 0 1 2 3 4 5 6

 Activities by the IMPACT Project at the University of North London, collated and rewritten by Ruth Merttens, Alan Newland and Susie Webb with additional material by Ellika McAuley, Kerry Carter, Ros Leather and Tina Hawley.

Editor Jane Bishop
Assistant editor Sally Gray
Designer Louise Belcher
Series designer Anna Oliwa
Illustrations ~~Gloria~~
Cover illustration Hardlines, Charlbury, Oxford

Designed using Aldus Pagemaker
Printed in Great Britain by Ebenezer Baylis and Son Ltd, Worcester

British Library Cataloguing-in-Publication Data
A catalogue record for this book is available from the British Library.

ISBN 0-590-53379-7

All rights reserved. This book is sold subject to the condition that it shall not, by way of trade or otherwise, be lent, hired out or otherwise circulated without the publisher's prior consent in any form of binding or cover other than that in which it is published and without a similar condition, including this condition, being imposed upon the subsequent purchaser.

No part of this publication may be reproduced, stored in a retrieval system, or transmitted, in any form or by any means, electronic, mechanical, photocopying, recording or otherwise, without the prior permission of the publisher. This book remains copyright, although permission is granted to copy pages 8 to 27; 30 to 57 and 60 to 95 for classroom distribution and use only in the school which has purchased the book, or by the teacher who has purchased this book and in accordance with the CLA licensing agreement. Photocopying permission is given for purchasers only and not for borrowers of books from any lending service.

CONTENTS

Introduction	5

Three year olds

Teachers' notes	6–7
Road signs	8
At home	9
Through my window	10
Mary had a…?	11
Crispy, crunchy crackers	12
Who lives in your house?	13
Olympic toy-stand	14
This book belongs to me!	15
Teddy's adventures	16
Private property	17
My favourite colours	18
Rainbows	19
Hearts	20
Kisses	21
Listening walk	22
Personalised place mat	23
Waves	24
Blowing bubbles	25
Stick in the mud!	26
Hi!	27

Four year olds

Teachers' notes	28–29
Same or different?	30
Carrying an orange!	31
Clothes on!	32
My name	33
Car number plates	34
My favourite pet	35
My favourite TV character	36
My reading book	37
Lift the flap	38
A leaf	39
Noises in the night	40
Home sweet home	41
Morning, afternoon and night…	42
Match my name	43
Firework fantasy	44
My best friends	45
Alphabet fruit and veg	46
Alphabet clothes	47
My room	48
Kidnapped!	49
My favourite sweets	50
I am an acrostic!	51
I love juice!	52
Alphabet colours	53
Alphabet toys	54
My favourite room	55
Jazzy name	56
In my home	57

Five year olds

Teachers' notes	58–59
Humpty Dumpty	60
Writing straight letters	61
Curly letters	62
Doing words	63
Alliteration	64
Shopping list	65

impact
WRITING HOMEWORK

CONTENTS

The 'at' family	66	Night work	82
Moving toys	67	Alphabet furniture	83
What can it be?	68	Hall of fame	84
Can you do this?	69	Holiday meals	85
Tick-tock says the clock!	70	Short names	86
Party invitations	71	In the future	87
Favourite fruit	72	Chips detective	88
Describing fabrics	73	Smart detective	89
Goldilocks	74	TV stars	90
Headlines	75	Fantasy holiday	91
Tea for hungry giants!	76	Alphabet TV guide	92
Please come to my party	77	Write yourself a letter!	93
Picture dictionary	78	Howdy partner!	94
All the fun of the fair	79	Shelf stacker	95
Days of the week	80		
I remember when…	81	Afterword	96

impact
WRITING HOMEWORK

IMPACT INTRODUCTION

IMPACT books are designed to help teachers involve parents in children's learning to write. Through the use of interesting and specially developed writing tasks, parents can encourage and support their child's efforts as they become confident and competent writers.

The shared writing programme is modelled on the same process as the IMPACT shared maths which encompasses a non-traditional approach to homework.

This is outlined in the following diagram:

> The teacher selects a task based on the work she is doing in class. The activity may relate to the children's work in a particular topic, to the type of writing they are engaged in or to their reading.

⇩

> The teacher prepares the children for what they have to do at home. This may involve reading a particular story, playing a game or having a discussion with the children about the task.

⇩

> The children take home the activity, and share it with someone at home. This may be an older brother/sister, a parent or grandparent or any other friend or relation.

> The parents and children respond to the activity by commenting in an accompanying diary or notebook.
> * This mechanism provides the teacher with valuable feedback.

⇩

> The teacher uses what was done at home as the basis for follow-up work in class/nursery. This may involve further writing, drawing, reading, discussion.

The activities in this book have been designed to enable children to develop and expand their writing skills in conversation with those at home. Where possible the activities reflect the context of the home rather than the school/nursery, and draw upon experiences and events from out-of-school situations.

Shared activities – or homework with chatter!

Importantly, the activities are designed to be shared. Unlike traditional homework, where the child is expected to 'do it alone' and not to have help, with IMPACT they are encouraged – even required – to find someone to talk to and share the activity with. With each task we say the following should be true:
- something is said;
- something is written;
- something is read.

Sometimes the main point of the IMPACT activity is the discussion – and so we try to encourage parents to see that the task involves more than just doing some writing. It is very important that teachers go through the task carefully with the children so that they know what to do. Clearly not all the children, or parents, will be able to read the instructions in English and so this preparation is crucial if the children are to be able to share the activity. The sheet often acts more as a backup or a prompt than a recipe.

Diaries

The shared writing works by involving parents in their children's learning. The IMPACT diaries are a crucial part of this process. They provide a mechanism by means of which an efficient parent-teacher-dialogue is established. These diaries enable teachers to obtain valuable feedback both about children's performances in relation to specific activities and about the tasks themselves. Parents are able to alert the teacher to any matter of concern or pleasant occurrences, and nothing is left to come as a big surprise or a horrible shock in the end of year report. It is difficult to exaggerate the importance of the IMPACT diaries. The OFSTED inspectors and HMI have highly commended their effectiveness in helping to raise children's achievements and in developing a real partnership with parents.
* See the Afterword (page 96) for details of where to obtain these.

Parent friendly

It is important for the success of the IMPACT Shared Writing that parents are aware of both the purpose and the extent of the work. This can be done by sending home a letter and arranging a meeting for all the parents to attend, where they can find out your plans and hopes for this joint venture. Specific points for discussion may include the rationale behind the developmental approach to writing, which encourages emergent writing or the use of invented spellings. Care has to be taken to share the philosophy behind such approaches with parents, and to select activities which will not assume that parents are as familiar with the implications as educators. You will get lots of support when parents see that they are helping their children to become happy and successful writers!

To facilitate this process, each activity contains a note to parents which helps to make it clear what the purpose of the activity is, and how they can best help. The activities also contain hints to help parents share the activity enjoyably and effectively. Sometimes the hints contain ideas, or starting points, or they may be examples of how to complete the task.

It is always important to bear in mind that parents can, and sometimes should, do things differently at home. The most successful partnerships between home and school recognise both the differences and the similarities in each other's endeavours. Ensure that the work that the children do with their parents at home is always valued.

Early years activities

This book has been especially designed to provide teachers and nursery/playgroup leaders with activities which supply suitable writing tasks for parents and children to share.
They provide:
- a selection of activities which parents will see as educationally valuable;
- a means of helping children to develop early writing skills and knowledge.

Planning

The shared writing activities are divided into three sections according to age: three, four and five year olds. There are two pages of teachers' notes relating to the individual activities at the beginning of each section. Try to send home the same sheet with all the children. Sometimes it may be necessary to add individual points or comments to certain sheets to facilitate the activity.

Teachers' Notes
THREE YEAR OLDS

Road signs Encourage the children to look at displays and print around your setting. Help them to 'read' and interact with signs. Talk about colours and what they might mean.

At home Use this information in a topic on 'Ourselves'. Help the children to count how many liked to play in the garden, help wash the car and so on. Display the results as a bar chart.

Through my window Use this activity to generate a discussion about what the children like or don't like about their local environment.

Mary had a...? Use this activity to do some work on colour with the children. Help the children to make pictures of a

purple parrot, a green gorilla and so on. Use the pictures to make a colour display.

Crispy, crunchy crackers Display all the empty packets and cartons with the caption, 'We can read all of these'. Talk about the colours used for different flavours, for example, 'Are all salt and vinegar flavoured crisps in the same colour bag?'.

Who lives in your house? Use this activity to help settle the children in. Look at the children's pictures and use the opportunity to talk about different types of families, being sensitive to the children's backgrounds.

Olympic toy-stand Create lots of opportunities for children to discuss choices and put them in an order of preference, ranking first, second, third: such as books of the week, favourite activities and favourite meals. Remember to offer limited choices to put in rank order and suggest things that need to be discussed and preferred rather than simply ranking size, weight, height and speed which is a different kind of activity.

This book belongs to me! Make book or folder covers and name labels with tactile letters of the children's names using felt, velvet, sand paper, reflective silver paper, dimpled paper and so on. Work with the children to make some templates with the letters of their names cut-out so they can draw inside them and use them to label their own books and possessions. Make book marks from a strip of card with the child's name repeatedly printed or written down the card to make a pattern.

Teddy's adventures Use the children's stories to produce a popular group book. Use the opportunity to introduce the days of the week which could lead into further comprehension work, such as, 'When did Teddy go to Cara's house?', or 'What did Teddy do on Tuesday at Myron's house?'.

Private property Provide labels in class for the children to label items of belongings like trays, lunch boxes and clothing. Make badges and hats with names on and decorate them. Design some toy ID cards or passports with names and photos.

My favourite colours Choose a different colour each week to make a display with a variety of toys the children have painted in the chosen colour. Create a zig-zag book with each page a different colour with coloured drawings of toys, familiar objects and foods. Label each page with the colour translated in to languages such as: red, *rouge*, *rosso* and so on.

Rainbows Paint an enormous rainbow in the classroom. Talk about the colours as you paint them (or mix them). Ask each child to paint a picture of one animal to go under the rainbow, try to ensure each one is different and label it with a name. Discuss the first letters of the animals'

names, sounding them out and saying the letter name.

Hearts/Kisses Make a class book of all the children's pictures. Encourage each child to write a caption to go with their picture or copy down their dictation. Discuss other symbols like smiley faces. Make a card for someone who cares for them using some of the symbols.

Listening walk Make a series of sound pictures on the wall. These can be big paintings such as traffic (with lots of different vehicles), birds (showing different kinds) or other animals and people. Make lists of words to go with each picture (car, van, lorry, truck, bus and so on). Write them on large coloured card and display them around the picture.

Personalised place mat Send the children home with a piece of card with a round shape marked on to it. The place mats can be covered in clear plastic and displayed before the children take them back home. Do some simple cookery or baking to go on the place mats. Extend the activity by making matching coaster sets.

Waves Make a 'wavy' display with waves and water and wind and with other 'w' words highlighted. Match 'w's' with words around the class and with names. Compile a list of 'w' words and display some artefacts that begin with 'w'.

Blowing bubbles Learn the song 'I'm forever blowing bubbles'. Talk about which letters have 'bubbles' in them and which have 'burst bubbles' in them such as: book, cook and look, or begin with a bubble like orange or open. Mix washing-up liquid with powder paint to make some bubble pictures, or use drinking straws to print bubbles and write some 'o' words into them.

Stick in the mud! Make a huge display with 'sticks in the mud' and shape letters around them. Help the children to think of objects that begin with their stick letters such as, b: ball. Make lists of words and pictures to go with them. Create some different pictures with small sticks or pieces of play dough.

Hi! Talk about different ways of saying hello and how people greet each other in different languages. Draw pictures of people the children like to greet and write their names and a greeting on the picture. Make letters and words with lollipop sticks, used matches and play dough.

To the helper:

● Discuss the meaning of the signs and the colours that are used.

This activity encourages children to interpret symbols and colours to convey meaning.

_____and
child

_____
helper(s)

_____
did this activity together

8   Early years activities

Road signs

Look out for some road signs.

● Draw any that you see on your way home.

impact WRITING HOMEWORK

At home

● Draw a picture about what you like doing best at home. Make up a caption to go with it.

To the helper:

● Model the writing for your child and show them how you form the letters.
● Help them to think of a suitable caption.

The children will be developing their skills of using pictures and words to convey information. In our group we will talk about the pictures and count how many children like to play outside, or help with the cooking.

_____and
child

_____
helper(s)

_____

did this activity together

Early years activities

To the helper:

- Before your child starts to draw, discuss what they can see. Is it always there?
- Talk about the colours and numbers of cars, doors and trees and any people they can see.

This activity will help children to become more observant of their locality. It will also help them to develop a geographical vocabulary which they can use in discussions about their local environment.

_____ and
child

_____
helper(s)

_____
did this activity together

Through my window

- Draw a picture of what you can see through a window in your home.

Mary had a ...?

Do you know the nursery rhyme, Mary had a little lamb?

- Think of a different animal for Mary.
- Draw a picture of it and write its name.

To the helper:

- Help your child to use the same initial letter sound to describe the animal. For instance, an enormous elephant or a large lizard.

This activity encourages children to focus on a particular letter sound.

_____ and
child

_____
helper(s)

_____
did this activity together

Early years activities

To the helper:

- Talk about the words, letters and pictures on the packet. How do we know what is inside the packet?

This activity helps children to understand the use of words and pictures to give us information.

_____ and
child

_____
helper(s)

_____
did this activity together

12   Early years activities

Crispy, crunchy crackers

- Find an empty carton or packet of your favourite crisps, cereal or biscuits and bring it in.

Can you read some of the words on the packet?

impact WRITING HOMEWORK

Who lives in your house?

- Draw all the people who live with you and write down their names.

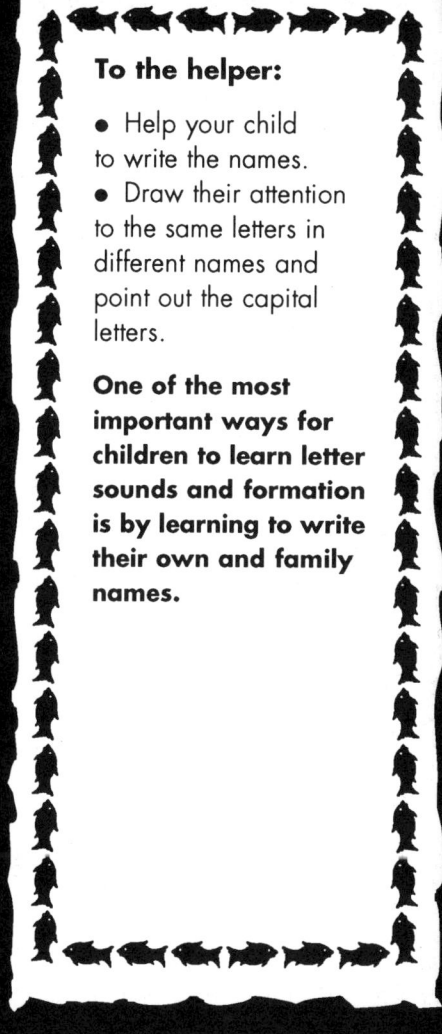

To the helper:
- Help your child to write the names.
- Draw their attention to the same letters in different names and point out the capital letters.

One of the most important ways for children to learn letter sounds and formation is by learning to write their own and family names.

_____and

child

_____

helper(s)

_____

did this activity together

Early years activities

To the helper:

- Help your child to consider what their favourite toy is and why they like it more than another. This will help them to order their thoughts.
- Write out letters and words slowly so your child can see how the shapes of the letters are formed.
- Spell out the names so your child will begin to learn the letters.

This activity introduces children to writing lists and using writing to order their thoughts and priorities.

_____and
child

_____
helper(s)

_____
did this activity together

14   Early years activities

Olympic toy-stand

What are your three favourite toys?

- Draw a picture of the gold, silver and bronze medal winners in your favourite toy Olympics!
- Write their names underneath.

impact WRITING HOMEWORK

This book belongs to me!

- Write your name on the labels below and decorate them.

You can cut them out and use them to stick on the inside of your books so everyone will know who they belong to.

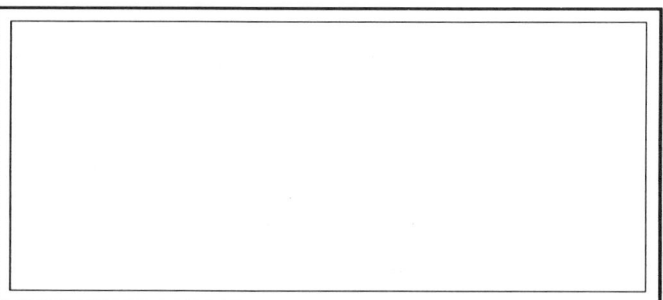

To the helper:

- Show your child the letters of their name by writing it out for them if they are not sure.
- Encourage them to learn how to shape their own letters rather than copy over those you have written.

Learning to write one's own name is usually a child's first achievement in writing and can be a source of great interest and motivation for them to write more.

_____and
child

_____
helper(s)

_____

did this activity together

To the helper:

- Each child in our group is having a turn to take Teddy home and write about his adventures!
- Help your child to talk about what Teddy has been doing. Show them how you write down the words that they say.

This shared writing activity shows the children that they can make up a story and be an 'author'. In our group we will make the children's stories into a book.

_____and
child

_____
helper(s)

_____
did this activity together

Teddy's adventures

Please look after Teddy tonight.

- Draw a picture and ask your helper to help you write about what happens to Teddy in your home.

16   Early years activities

impact WRITING HOMEWORK

Private property

- Write your name on these things so that everyone knows who they belong to.

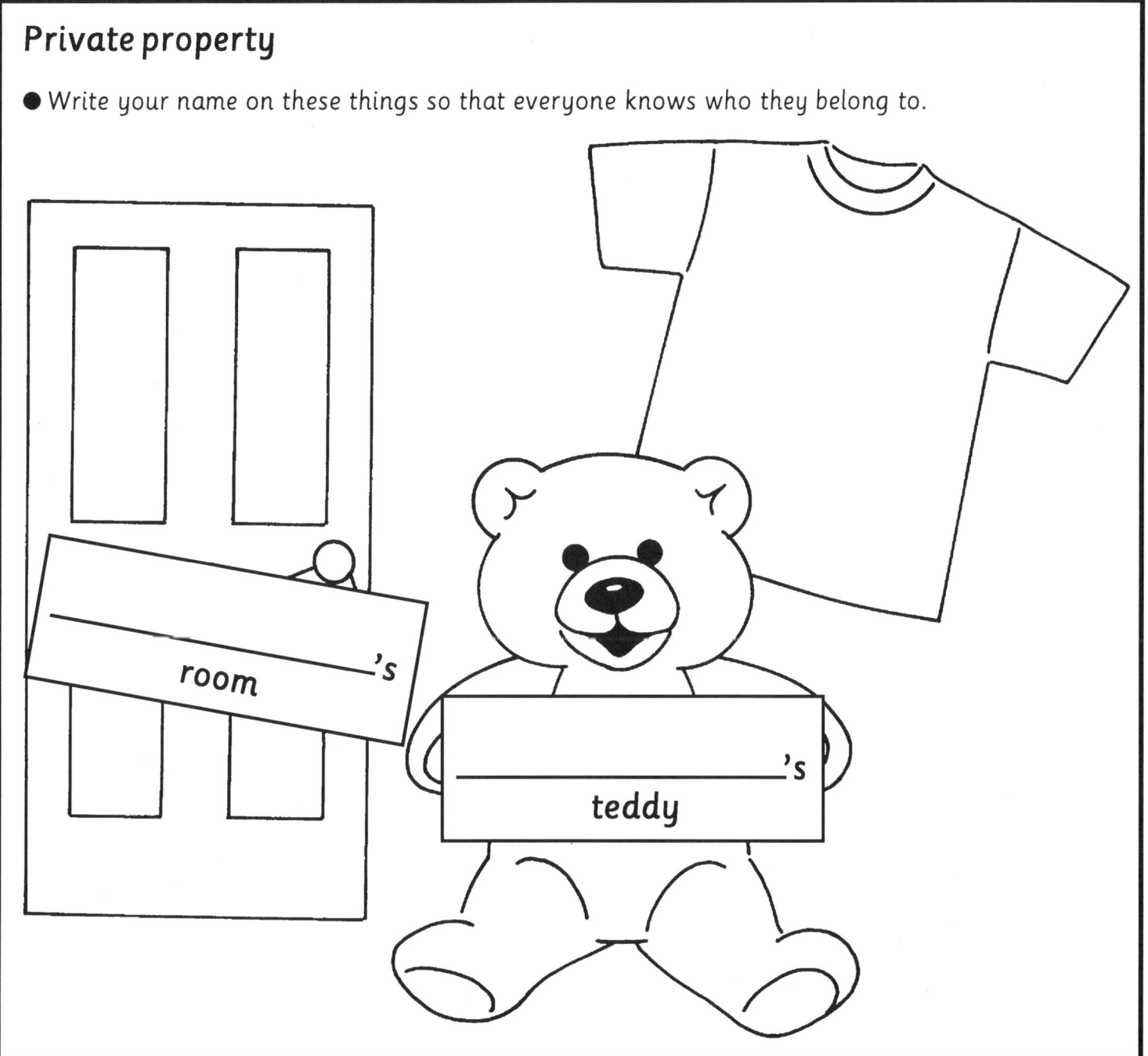

To the helper:

- Show your child the letters of their name by writing it out for them if they are not sure.
- Encourage them to learn and shape their own letters rather than copy over those you have written.

Learning to write one's own name is usually a child's first achievement in writing and can be a source of great interest and motivation for them to write more.

_____ and
child

_____
helper(s)

_____
did this activity together

Early years activities

To the helper:

- Discuss with your child what their favourite colour is and why. This will help them give order to their thoughts.
- Write out the letters slowly so your child can see how the shapes of the letters are formed.
- Spell out the names of colours so your child will begin to learn the letters.

This activity introduces children to writing lists and using writing to order their thoughts and priorities.

_____ and
child

_____
helper(s)

_____
did this activity together

18   Early years activities

My favourite colours

What are your favourite colours?

- Colour in these teddy bears and write the colours you have chosen for them underneath.

impact WRITING HOMEWORK

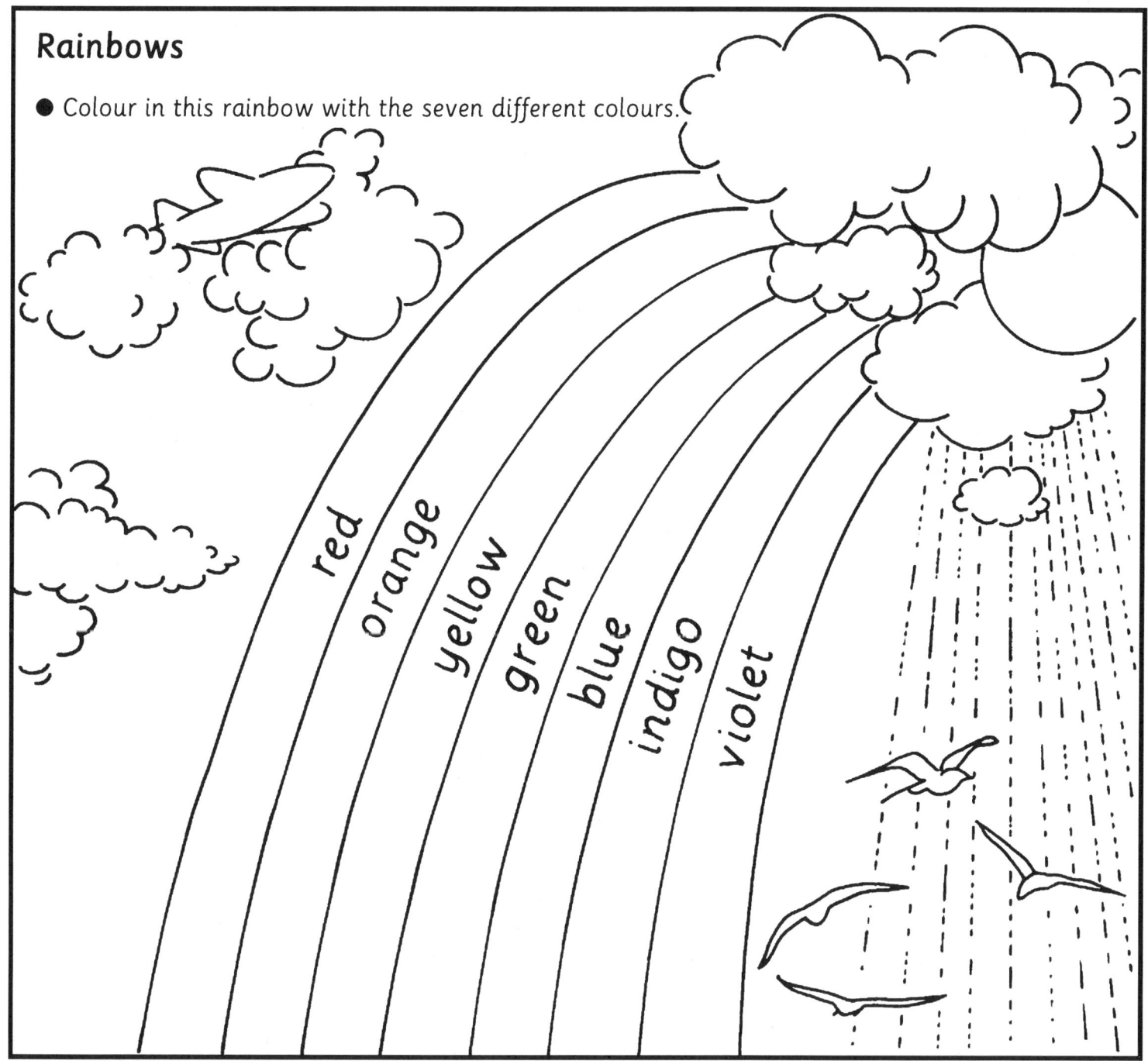

Rainbows

- Colour in this rainbow with the seven different colours.

red, orange, yellow, green, blue, indigo, violet

To the helper:

- Help your child to choose their colours and to put them in the right order on their rainbow.

This activity will help children to recognise and learn their colours. It will also help them to develop skills of hand to eye co-ordination in preparation for more precise writing.

_____ and
child

_____
helper(s)

_____
did this activity together

Early years activities

To the helper:

- Talk about who the child wants to draw. Perhaps they can draw someone they don't see very often like a grandparent or relative?

This activity will help children realise that marks and symbols on the page mean something. This is essential preparation to writing.

_____ and
child

_____
helper(s)

_____

did this activity together

20   Early years activities

Hearts

- Draw some hearts.
- Draw a picture of someone you love.

impact WRITING HOMEWORK

Kisses

- Draw some kisses on the page.
- Draw a picture of someone you would like to kiss!

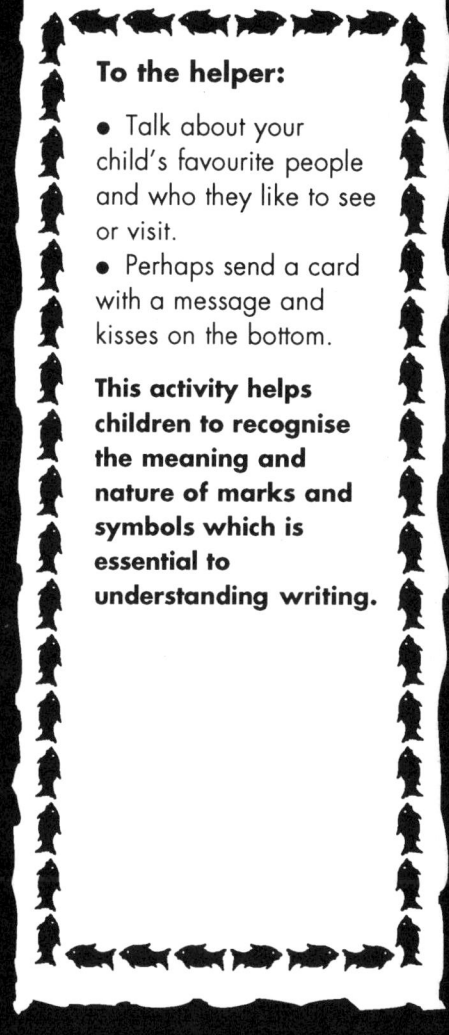

To the helper:

- Talk about your child's favourite people and who they like to see or visit.
- Perhaps send a card with a message and kisses on the bottom.

This activity helps children to recognise the meaning and nature of marks and symbols which is essential to understanding writing.

_____and
child

_____
helper(s)

_____

did this activity together

impact WRITING HOMEWORK

Early years activities

To the helper:

- Help your child to pay attention to the sounds they can hear on their walk. Are there any unusual or special sounds?

This activity introduces the children to the idea that writing is a collection of symbols that represent sounds.

_____and

child

_____

helper(s)

_____

did this activity together

Early years activities

Listening walk

Go for a walk with your helper.

- Write down or draw all the things you hear.

impact WRITING HOMEWORK

Personalised place mat

- Make your very own place mat by using the round part of the card provided.
- Think about what you can draw or write on it.

To the helper:

- Help your child to work on their mat and make it look special. Ask them to write their name on it somewhere.
- We shall cover them with clear plastic at school and send them home again so they can be used.

Making things like this helps children to see the reasons for learning to write.

_____and
child

_____
helper(s)

_____
did this activity together

impact WRITING HOMEWORK

Early years activities

To the helper:

- Help your child to draw a zig-zag line like a string of w's.
- Help them with the formation of the shapes of waves and ships.

This activity will help the children to improve their hand to eye co-ordination and prepare them for the formation of alphabetic shapes. It will also help them with letter recognition.

_____ and
child

_____
helper(s)

_____
did this activity together

24   Early years activities

Waves

- Draw a ship on these waves.

W is a wavy letter.

- Try drawing some more waves and ships to sail on them.

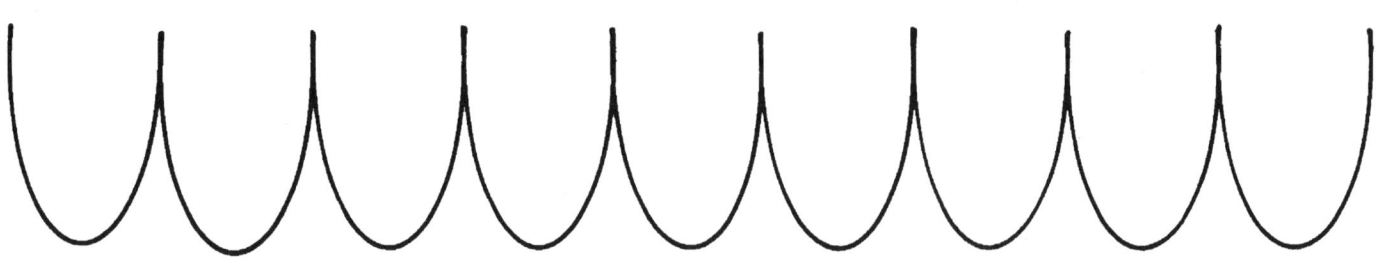

impact WRITING HOMEWORK

Blowing bubbles

- Draw lots of circle bubbles.

Lots of letters have circles in them.

- Draw a bubble and then make it into a letter! How many can you do?

To the helper:

- Help your child to form the bubble circular shapes.
- When you have done some, turn them into letters such as: e, g, d, a, q, p, o, b.
- Does anyone in the family have a name that begins with one of these letters.

This activity will help children to start to draw and recognise letters in a way which is fun.

_____ and
child

_____
helper(s)

_____
did this activity together

To the helper:

- Help your child to arrange the sticks.
- Suggest some letters that have 'sticks' in them for example, p, k and n. Help with the formation of the letters.
- Talk about 'stick' letters in names of the family members.

This activity helps children to form basic letter shapes and develop hand to eye co-ordination in preparation for more precise writing later.

_____and

child

_____

helper(s)

_____

did this activity together

Stick in the mud!

Lots of letters have sticks in them!

- Draw a line of sticks in the mud.
- Make some of your sticks in to letters.

Perhaps there's a letter there that's in your name?

Hi!

Hi is a short way of saying hello!

- Arrange some knives and forks or chopsticks to make a word.

impact WRITING HOMEWORK

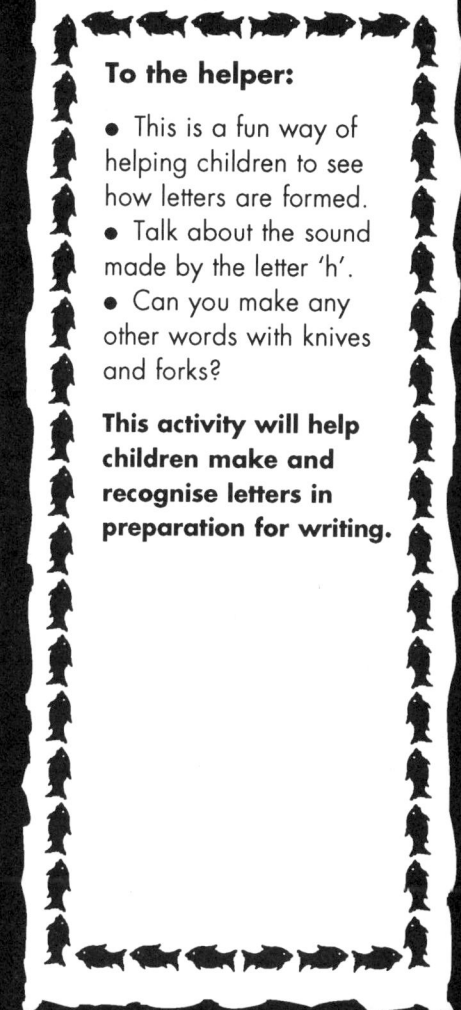

To the helper:

- This is a fun way of helping children to see how letters are formed.
- Talk about the sound made by the letter 'h'.
- Can you make any other words with knives and forks?

This activity will help children make and recognise letters in preparation for writing.

_____and
child

_____
helper(s)

_____
did this activity together

Early years activities 27

Teachers' Notes
FOUR YEAR OLDS

Same or different? Choose two stories to read to the children such as *The Little Red Hen* (Traditional) and *The Little Yellow Chicken*, Big All Together Books, Sunshine Series (Heinemann) and ask children to think of things that are the same and different about the two stories. Prepare two sheets of paper, one labelled 'similarities', the other labelled 'differences'. Write down the children's ideas on to the sheets as they think of them. The children will probably find it easier to think of differences.

Carrying an orange! Give children an opportunity to test their carriers. Provide a low table and sit the children in a semi-circle. Ask each child to demonstrate their model and discuss how it works. Children who have been unable to make an orange

carrier at home may like to have a go with you, using reclaimed materials or construction apparatus.

Clothes on! Collect some articles of clothing and make labels for them. Ask the children to suggest an order for dressing. Pin the clothes up in the agreed order. Using Blu-Tack ask the children to place the labels in the correct position. Remove the labels or mix them up and ask for volunteers to replace them correctly.

My name Make a class book with the children's names arranged in alphabetical order. Add pictures of toys to each page. Help the children to arrange themselves in alphabetical order. In unison, say the name and letter sound for each of the letters.

Car number plates Ask the children to write their car number plate letters on separate pieces of paper. Sit the children in a circle, holding their letters. Ask each child in turn to come and put their letters out in alphabetical order. It will help if you place an alphabet frieze on the floor for the children to match up their letters with. Talk about the upper and lower case versions of the letters. Practise saying the names of the letters and the letter sounds together.

My favourite pet Make a collection of pet pictures, names and noises. Children can match these before they stick their words into a class book. Display the book, so that the children can read the book in spare moments.

My favourite TV character Read a favourite book, ask the children to suggest why some characters are more important than others in the book. Write their ideas on large sheets of paper with fat felt-tipped pens. Read them together and pin them up with a copy of the book.

My reading book Read a favourite book and discuss the beginning, middle and end of the story. Ask the children to think of alternative endings to the story. Give each child a piece of paper folded into three. Ask them to write a story on the paper, writing the beginning in the first section, the middle in the second and the ending in the third section.

Lift the flap Make a display of the children's work. Include a selection of 'lift the flap' books that you have shared with the class, alongside the children's work. Talk about which ones they have enjoyed the most and why. Write a class 'lift the flap' book together. Choose an idea such as hiding the nouns in the story with a flap showing the picture. Help older children to write the story on the computer using a large font. This book will become a class favourite being read over and over again.

A leaf Compile a list of words to describe both sides of the leaf. They are often opposites: hairy – smooth; dull – shiny; dark green – light green. Draw the children's attention to the fact that some of the words are opposites. Lay out some leaves in front of the children. Describe one of the leaves and see if the children can work out which one you are talking about. When you have modelled this a few times invite some of the children to do the same, describing a leaf for the others to guess.

Noises in the night Use this activity when teaching the children about day and night and time cycles. Read the story *Peace At Last* by Jill Murphy (Picturemac) to introduce the activity.

Home sweet home Talk about the children's pictures together. Identify the variety of houses that the children have brought in and use the information to do some simple data handling work. Create a large scale map of the local area, showing the different types of houses to introduce the children to the purpose of maps.

Morning, afternoon and night... This activity will provide the opportunity to discuss the patterns of the children's days. Extend this work by discussing events that only happen on specific days of the week at specific times.

Match my name Create opportunities to work alongside the children to do name matching searches around the room or in catalogues, brochures and magazines. For example, look through a mail order catalogue to find an item that begins with the same letter as a child's name, cut it out and paste it in to a name matching book. Use other categories to match with initial letter names. Match names to adjectives like Angry Annie and so on.

Firework fantasy Display the completed work as words exploding out of an enormous firework. Use the opportunity to reinforce safety around fireworks.

My best friends Each child can undertake a project of making a three or four page 'Best Friend Book'. This could include photos of their best friends, with names and captions written underneath and drawings of their favourite games, pastimes and things they do together. Make the front cover letters from a tactile material like felt or dimpled paper.

Alphabet fruit and veg Create a class alphabet to include everybody's contributions. Work together to make lists that begin with a particular letter. For example: B – biscuits, beans, berries, bread and butter. Do some alphabet cookery with the children, making biscuits, toast or sandwiches in the children's initial letter shapes. Use potatoes and other vegetables to make prints of the children's names.

Alphabet clothes Create a fantastic display of alphabet clothes from the children's suggestions. Ask the children to draw or paint pictures of the clothes and ask for their help in arranging the pictures in alphabetical order. For example, anorak, boots, cardigan, duffle coat and so on. Play some I-Spy games with the display. Make some lists of other clothes beginning with the same letters.

My room Make a large display of room name plates cut out or made up into three-dimensional signs from various newspaper, magazine and print fonts. Make a selection of room name plates to label areas in the room or around the school. Use tactile materials such as velvet, velcro and sandpaper.

Kidnapped! Invite the children to draw themselves or use an enlarged photocopied photo to make 'Kidnapped' or 'Wanted' posters. Write names and captions underneath using newspaper or magazine print. The children might also like to use the various fonts on word processing packages.

My favourite sweets Create lots of opportunities for the children to discuss choices. Have discussions about favourite foods and give the children practice in placing a limited selection of things in rank order. Suggest things that need to be discussed and preferred rather than ranking size, weight and so on which is a different kind of activity. Make rosettes for prizes in the 'Sweet Show'.

I am an acrostic! Make a class book of acrostic poems with all the contributions the children bring in, display some in large print. Create some other ways for the children to make acrostics from their names. For example with each letter of their name being used as a sweet brand, an item of clothing, a fruit or veg and so on.

I love juice! Do some simple juice-making in the class with the recipes the children bring in. Work alongside them to write out the ingredients, measures and methods. You can have tasting competitions and rank ordering of flavours awarding first, second and third prizes. 'Bottle' the juice and make your own special labels for the containers. Make a juice recipe book.

Alphabet colours Make a large rainbow or circle of primary colours and label them with the colour names, highlighting the initial letters. If you feel that the children are confident with the regular colour names, collect some colour cards from paint shops and hardware stores and introduce them to some lesser known names for colour varieties (crimson, emerald and vermillion for example). Make a zigzag book with each page a different colour with coloured drawings of toys, familiar objects and foods.

Alphabet toys Use the children's contributions to make lists of toys in alphabetical order and from these create a large display highlighting the initial letters of the toys' names. Use the display as a stimulus for playing games, such as I-Spy or Hangman.

My favourite room Use this activity in conjunction with a topic on homes. Have a discussion with the children about why homes are special and how they make us feel.

Jazzy name Use the children's names to create a huge collage of tactile jazzy names from sand paper, velvet, silk, felt, velcro and shiny reflective paper. This display will provide an excellent visual stimulus for the children and will encourage them to learn the letters of the alphabet in a meaningful context.

In my home Make a list of all the capital letters used. Have all the letters of the alphabet been used? Have any letters been used more than once? Work with small groups of children to match up the capital letters with their lower case equivalents.

To the helper:

- Choose two toys from the same category, such as two cars or two teddies. Your child will probably find it easier to identify differences rather than similarities.
- Write down your child's ideas for them and read back the sentences together.
- Encourage your child to choose their two favourite similarities and differences to bring in to share.

In all areas of the curriculum children are required to sort objects, stories, numbers and so on using different criteria.

_____ and
child

_____
helper(s)

_____
did this activity together

Early years activities

Same or different?

Look carefully at two of your favourite toys.

● Write down some things that are the same about them.

Can you find any differences too?

impact WRITING HOMEWORK

Carrying an orange!

Can you make something that will carry an orange?

You will need lots of reclaimed materials and other equipment such as boxes, lids, yoghurt pots, wire, adhesive, sticky tape and string.

- Make a list of the things you have used to make the carrier.

To the helper:

- Allow your child some time to experiment with the equipment before intervening. Once they have tried out some ideas, help them by making suggestions and modifying their plans.
- Ask your child to tell you what to write on the list of materials that they used.

This activity is excellent for helping your child to make decisions. It will also help them to learn how to overcome problems and to work co-operatively.

_____ and
child

_____
helper(s)

_____
did this activity together

To the helper:

- Suggest to your child that they lay out their clothes for the day. Talk with them about which thing comes first, second and so on.
- Help them to number and label their pictures.

This activity will help children to sequence and order everyday events.

_____and
child

_____
helper(s)

_____
did this activity together

Early years activities

Clothes on!

In what order do you put your clothes on in the morning?

- Draw pictures of your clothes showing the order in which you put them on.
- Label and number the different items.

impact WRITING HOMEWORK

My name

- Write your name clearly here.

Can you say the sound for each of the letters?

- Draw some toys that start with the same sounds as the letters in your name.

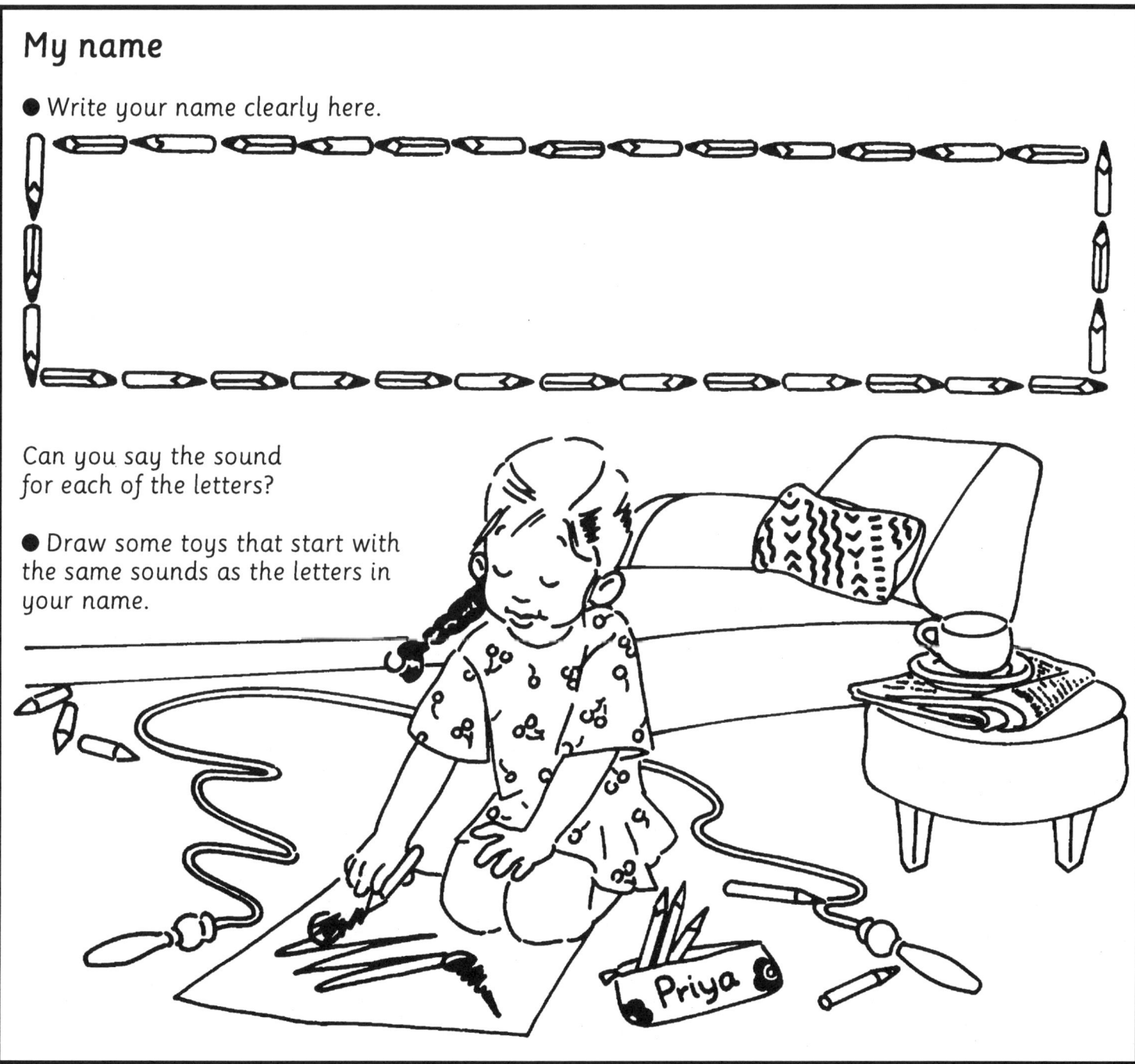

To the helper:

- Please help your child to use the letter sounds (for example 'a' for apple, not 'a' for apron) for this activity.
- Help your child to form the letters of their name correctly and use a capital letter to begin their name.
- Help them with suggestions for toys that have the same sounds as the letters in their names.

It is important for children to learn to distinguish the different sounds that letters make within a word.

_____ and
child

_____
helper(s)

_____

did this activity together

Early years activities

To the helper:

- Encourage your child to use the letter sound with the letter name (for example, 'e' as in Emma, not 'e' as in even).
- Write down the names your child has chosen for them to copy. Ensure that they are forming the letters correctly. Show them how you use capital letters to begin the name and then small letters.
- Play 'I spy' with your child to encourage them to hear the sound at the beginning of other words.

It is important for your child to hear sounds at the beginning of words. This is the first stage in independent writing.

_____and

child

_____

helper(s)

_____

did this activity together

Early years activities

Car number plates

- Look at your car or find a car to look at near to where you live.
- Draw the letters and numbers that you see into these spaces.

Can you think of any names that begin with the letters on the number plate?

- Ask your helper to help you write them down.

impact WRITING HOMEWORK

My favourite pet

● Draw your favourite pet here. It might be your own pet, or it might be one you would like to have.

Can you answer these questions?

My pet has _____ legs.

My pet is _____ in colour.

My pet has a coat of _____ .

My pet eats _____ .

My pet makes a _____ noise.

What do you like best about your pet?

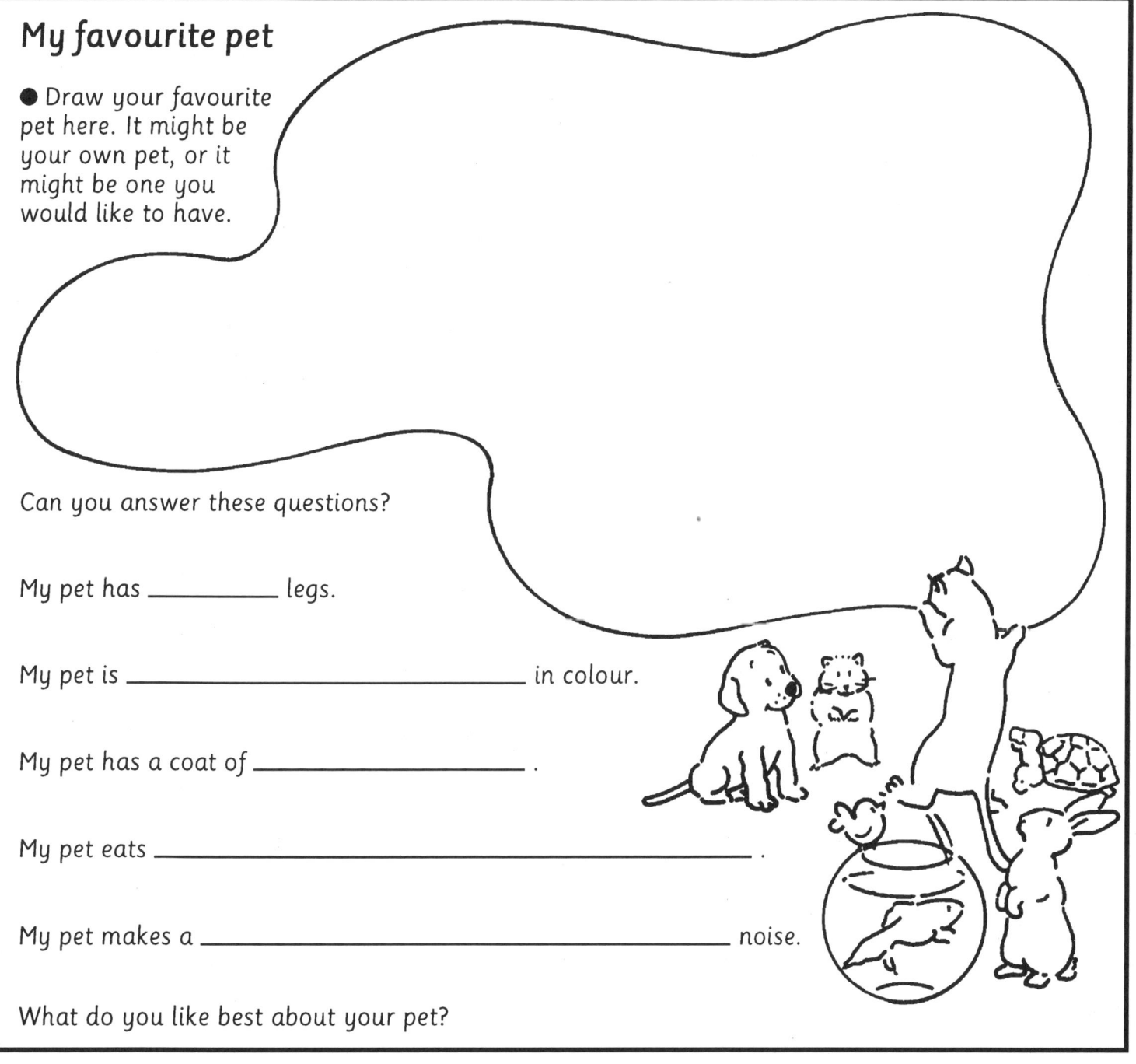

To the helper:

● Help your child to imagine their favourite pet, or to look closely at their own pet.
● Read the sentences together so that your child can think of suitable answers.
● Encourage your child to think up an exciting sentence about the pet.
● Please help your child with the writing. If appropriate write down your child's words for them to copy.

By thinking of appropriate endings to complete the sentences, your child will be learning how to read for meaning.

_____and
child

_____
helper(s)

_____

did this activity together

Early years activities

To the helper:

- Help your child to give reasons for their choice of character. Encourage them to think of as many different reasons as possible.
- Write the sentences on separate pieces of paper for your child. Ask them to watch how you make the letters.
- Read them together before asking your child to copy them.

This activity will encourage your child to think of characteristics that make something special. This will help them to enjoy reading and to have ideas for writing.

_____ and
child

_____
helper(s)

_____
did this activity together

36   **Early years activities**

My favourite TV character

- Draw your favourite TV character.

Can you think of three reasons why it is special to you?

- Write them down on a piece of paper.

impact WRITING HOMEWORK

My reading book

- Draw three pictures from your reading book.
- Ask someone at home to help you choose a page each from the beginning, middle and the end of your story and copy these pictures.

impact WRITING HOMEWORK

To the helper:

- Read the story together, talk about the beginning, middle and end of the story.
- Encourage your child to think of an alternative ending to the story. Can they think of a better way to end it?

All good stories have a beginning, middle and an end. Children will need lots of practice to perfect this model when they begin writing their own stories. Reading and discussing books which you have read helps this process.

_____and
child

_____
helper(s)

_____
did this activity together

Early years activities

To the helper:

- Read a 'lift the flap' book with your child if you have one (there are usually many examples in local libraries).
- Discuss with your child how the flaps help to make the story more exciting.

Children love surprises. Including a flap can capture your child's imagination and enthusiasm. This will encourage positive feelings towards reading and writing. Your child will also learn how to anticipate what might happen next in a story.

_____ and
child

_____
helper(s)

_____
did this activity together

Lift the flap

- Make a page that has a lift-up flap.
- Write or draw something under your flap.

A leaf

- Find a leaf.
- Look at it closely from all angles and draw it. Colour it in on both sides.
- Make a list of words to describe both sides of the leaf.

To the helper:

- Help your child to use their sense of touch, smell and sight to describe and compare the top and the underside of the leaf.
- Please write the list of words for your child to copy, showing them how you form the letters and discussing the sounds that the letters make.
- Try to encourage your child to be imaginative, for example: 'It feels like a hairy caterpillar'.

This activity will encourage the children to develop a 'describing' vocabulary when observing an object. This will help them when they begin to write stories.

_____ and
child

_____
helper(s)

_____
did this activity together

Early years activities

To the helper:

- Discuss with your child the sorts of noises they can hear in their bedroom.
- Help them to distinguish between the noises that they hear at night and those that they hear during the day. Which noises can they hear during the day and at night?
- Help your child with their writing.

This activity will help your child to differentiate between night and day.

_____and

child

_____

helper(s)

_____

did this activity together

40   Early years activities

Noises in the night

When you are tucked up in bed at night, what can you hear?

- Draw and name three noises that keep you awake at night.

impact WRITING HOMEWORK

Home sweet home

- Look very carefully at the outside of your home.
- Draw a picture of it and write down your address.

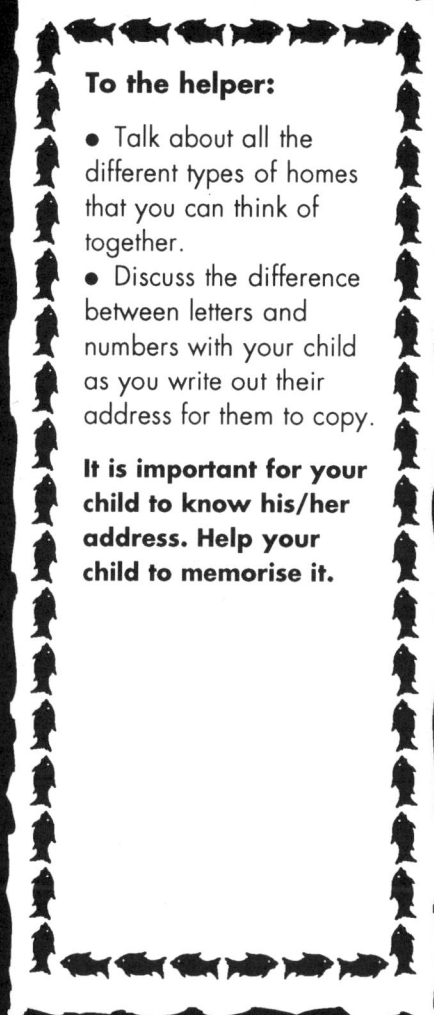

To the helper:

- Talk about all the different types of homes that you can think of together.
- Discuss the difference between letters and numbers with your child as you write out their address for them to copy.

It is important for your child to know his/her address. Help your child to memorise it.

_____ and
child

_____
helper(s)

_____
did this activity together

To the helper:
- Talk about your child's daily routines and help them to think of one thing that they always do for each of the three parts of the day.
- Divide a piece of paper into three sections and assist your child with the writing.

This activity will help children to place the events of the day in a sequence. It will help them to learn about the different parts to the day.

_____ and
child

_____
helper(s)

_____
did this activity together

Early years activities

Morning, afternoon and night...

● Draw and write about one thing that you do **every** morning, one every afternoon and one every night.

Match my name

Do you know which letter begins your name? What sound does it make?

- Find five pictures of other things that start with the same letter as your name.

To the helper:

- Help your child to identify the initial letter of their name by pointing to letters on food packaging and other things.
- Encourage them to trace the shape of raised letters with their finger on street signs, packaging and plaques.
- Help your child to find some pictures that begin with their letter. Look through magazines, catalogues and advertisements together.

Matching the initial letter of one's own name with other words is an important step in the beginnings of reading and writing.

_____and

child

_____

helper(s)

_____

did this activity together

impact WRITING HOMEWORK

Early years activities   43

To the helper:

- Discuss the sounds and sights of fireworks with your child. Help them to describe the fireworks in imaginative and descriptive language.
- Perhaps you could encourage your child to come up with some fantasy words and sounds.
- Help your child to write down their descriptions, you may like to scribe for them drawing their attention to the way you form the letters.

This activity uses an event that is familiar to children to develop their descriptive vocabulary.

_____ and
child

_____
helper(s)

_____
did this activity together

44 **Early years activities**

Firework fantasy

Do you like fireworks?

● Write some words to describe fireworks.

What do they sound and look like?

impact WRITING HOMEWORK

My best friends

Who are your best friends?

● Draw a picture of your two best friends and write their names underneath.

To the helper:

● Discuss with your chld who their favourite people are. Ask them to think about why they like them more than their other friends. This will help them give order to their thoughts.

● Write out letters and names slowly so your child can see how the shapes of the letters are formed. As you write, spell out the names so your child will begin to learn the letters.

This activity introduces children to writing lists and using writing to order their thoughts and priorities.

_____and
child

_____
helper(s)

_____
did this activity together

impact WRITING HOMEWORK

Early years activities 45

To the helper:

- Talk about the first letters of the names of fruit and vegetables with your child. Write out the alphabet for your child and help them to identify the relevant letters.
- Show them how to form the letters correctly, allowing them plenty of time to practise before they write the letters underneath their pictures

This activity helps the children learn the letters of the alphabet and gives them an opportunity to practise letter formation.

_____ and
child

_____
helper(s)

_____
did this activity together

Early years activities

Alphabet fruit and veg

How many letters of the alphabet do you know that begin the names of fruits and vegetables?

- Draw some fruit and vegetables here and write their letters underneath.

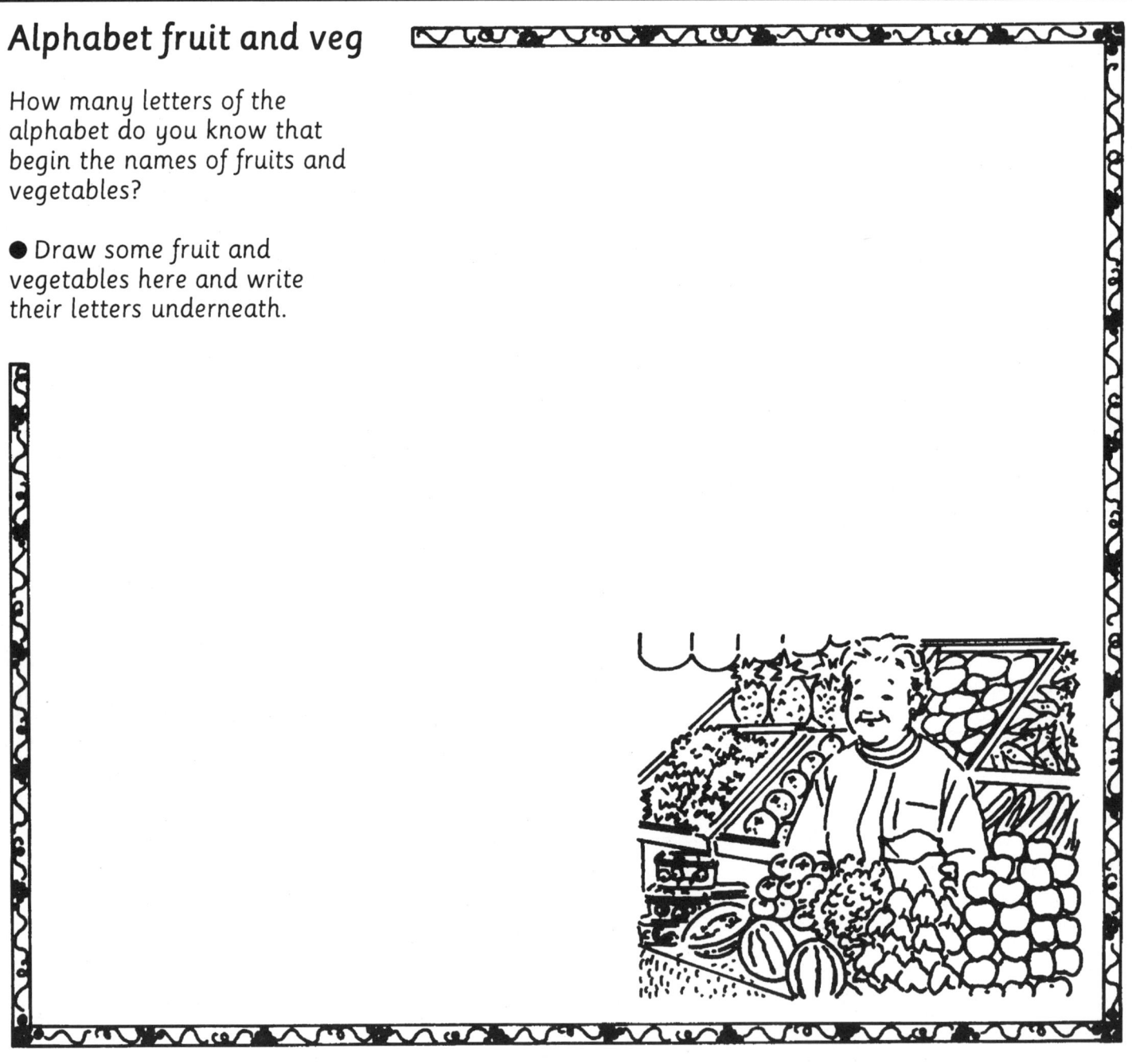

impact WRITING HOMEWORK

Alphabet clothes

How many letters of the alphabet do you know that begin the name of an item of clothing?

● Draw some of them and ask your helper to write down what they are underneath.

To the helper:

● Talk about the first letters of names and help your child find the letter in the alphabet list.
● As you write the name of the item of clothing focus on the first letter and help your child learn the letter name. Don't worry if you can't find 26!
● Write out letters and words slowly so your child can see how the shapes of the letters are formed.

This activity helps children learn the letters of the alphabet in a context in which they can bring their own knowledge to bear.

_____and
child

_____
helper(s)

_____

did this activity together

Early years activities

To the helper:

- Help your child to identify the letters in his/her name from headline print in an old newspaper or magazine.
- Help with cutting, sticking and arranging the letters if need be.
- Add an extra caption to the plaque such as 'Please Knock!' or 'Private Property!' if you like.

This activity helps your child to focus on identifying the letters of their name and using them in a purposeful way.

_____and
child

_____
helper(s)

_____
did this activity together

My room

● Cut out the letters of your name from the headlines of newspapers or magazines. Stick them on the room plaque below and decorate it.

Early years activities

impact WRITING HOMEWORK

Kidnapped!

● Cut out the letters of your name from newspaper or magazine headlines and stick them on a piece of paper to make a ransom note.

To the helper:

● Talk about ransom notes with your child and explain what they might have on them.
● Help your child to identify the letters in his/her name from headline print in an old newspaper.
● Help with cutting, sticking and arranging the letters if need be.
● Add an extra message to the ransom note for fun and crumple it up to make it look realistic.

This activity helps your child to focus on identifying the letters of their name and using them in a fun way.

_____and
child

_____
helper(s)

_____
did this activity together

Early years activities

To the helper:

- Discuss with your child what their favourite sweets are and why. This will help them give order to their thoughts.
- Write out the letters slowly so your child can see how the shapes of the letters are formed. Spell out the names of the sweets so your child will begin to learn the names of the letters and the sounds they make.

This activity introduces children to writing lists and using writing to order their thoughts and priorities.

_____ and
child

_____
helper(s)

_____
did this activity together

50   Early years activities

My favourite sweets

What are your favourite sweets?

● Draw pictures of your favourite sweets and write their names underneath.

impact WRITING HOMEWORK

I am an acrostic!

● Write your name down the side of the page and think of a word (or words) that describes you for each of the letters, like this:

Musical
Always laughing
Reads books
Caring
Unusual
Super!

To the helper:
● Talk about words which describe people and their attributes (adjectives).
● Try to come up with adjectives or phrases that are complimentary and make your child feel good about themselves (even if not all of them are entirely true!).
● You will need to help with the writing of the words and phrases but encourage your child to learn the spelling of their own name.

This activity, apart from helping to raise self esteem, is another way for children to learn the spelling of their own names.

_____and
child

_____
helper(s)

_____
did this activity together

impact WRITING HOMEWORK   **Early years activities**

To the helper:

- Help your child to sequence the actions for making a fruit drink. Talk about all the tasty fruity combinations that you can think of together.
- Help your child with writing the fruit names below the pictures. Write out the letters and words slowly so your child can see how the shapes of the letters are formed.

This activity introduces children to writing lists and using writing to order their thoughts and priorities.

_____ and

child

_____

helper(s)

_____

did this activity together

I love juice!

- Make a recipe for a delicious juice drink.
- Draw instructions for how to make it and label the ingredients.

52   Early years activities

impact WRITING HOMEWORK

Alphabet colours

- Say some colour names out loud.

Can you hear the letters they begin with?

- Look at the letters opposite, say the sounds they make. Now shade them in a colour to match that sound, for example colour the 'r' red.

To the helper:

- Talk about the first letters of colour names and help your child to find the letter in the group below.
- As your child colours in the letter the appropriate colour help them to remember the sound it makes.
- Ask them to trace the shape of the letter with their finger to learn how the letter is formed.

This activity helps children to learn the sounds of letters in the alphabet and helps them to relate the sounds to words that they are familiar with.

_____ and
child

_____
helper(s)

_____
did this activity together

Early years activities 53

To the helper:

- Say the names of your child's toys with them. Help them to hear the sound that their first letter makes.
- Help your child to write the letters that they need (you may need to remind them of the way that the letter looks) and encourage them to write the letters carefully underneath the drawings of their toys.

This activity helps children to learn the letters of the alphabet in a context that is meaningful to them.

_____and
child

_____
helper(s)

_____
did this activity together

Alphabet toys

- Choose five of your toys.

Do you know what letters they start with? Are they all different or are some the same?

- Draw your toys and write their letters underneath.

My favourite room

● Draw your favourite room at home and label the things in it.

To the helper:
● Talk about the rooms at home and discuss the things that are found in each room.
● Help your child to discuss why they have chosen a particular room: does it make them feel safe? Does it contain their toys?
● Help your child to write the name of the room and the labels.

This activity introduces the children to the idea of using writing to label objects.

_____and
child

_____
helper(s)

_____
did this activity together

Early years activities

To the helper:

- Use a different label or package for each letter of your child's name. Experiment with different arrangements before sticking them down.
- Focus on the names of letters and the sounds they make.
- Look at the way that even the same letters may have different shapes, styles and sizes from one food packet to the next.

This activity will help children become familiar with letter shapes and sounds and the variety of styles in which they are printed (called fonts).

_____and
child

_____
helper(s)

_____
did this activity together

Jazzy name

- Cut out the letters of your name from food packages. Use empty cereal packets, tin labels, left over pizza boxes or fast food wrappers. Stick them on the name panel below and make it as colourful and jazzy as you can!

56 Early years activities

impact WRITING HOMEWORK

In my home

- Make a list of all the people who live with you.

- Make the sound of the beginning letter in each name and draw a picture to match the sound.

To the helper:

- Help your child to remember all the people who live in their home.
- Help them with the names they can't spell and show them how to write out the other names, forming the letters carefully and beginning each name with a capital letter.
- Listen for the initial letter sounds together and help your child to choose a picture to draw to match the sound.

This activity will help the children to associate letters with their sounds. It will also provide an opportunity to practise letter formation.

_____ and
child

_____
helper(s)

_____
did this activity together

Early years activities

Teachers' Notes
FIVE YEAR OLDS

Humpty Dumpty Ask the children to make a big Humpty Dumpty picture. Display the rhyme alongside. Encourage the children to read the poem in unison as you point to each word in turn. Place the words or sentences of the poem in an envelope nearby. Encourage the children to rearrange the words to match the poem.

Writing straight letters Begin making a book with the straight letter family. Remind the children that all the straight letter family begin at the top and the pencil goes straight down. Draw the letters with a variety of media, such as finger paints, sand and with paint. Make an I-Spy book by drawing objects that begin with the letter on the relevant page.

Curly letters Make a curly letter display using painted letters. Write some alliterative sentences with the children. For example: the curly coated cat caught catkins on her coat. Read these sentences in unison until the children are familiar with the vocabulary. The children can then be asked to read particular sentences or find individual words.

Doing words Gather the children together and ask them to read their favourite sentence. Vary the activity by

asking the children to omit the doing word and asking the other children to guess what it might be. Extend the activity by encouraging the children to write an adverb to describe their verbs.

Alliteration Read *The Nickle Nackle Tree* by Lynley Dodd (out of print) to the children, or use another story that has plenty of alliterative phrases. Ask the children to spot the alliterative phrases in the story. Make a book of the children's own alliterative sentences.

Shopping list Children love making lists. Ask them to make an alphabetical order shopping list for food. Can the children find food for each letter of the alphabet? Which letters are very difficult or impossible?

The 'at' family Provide the children with a set of ten cards with the letters 'at' written on them and a set of alphabet cards. Encourage the children to make as many 'at' words as possible. Ask the children to work in pairs, reading the word and then writing it without copying. Make other sets of cards with different endings such as 'an', 'am', 'ag' and so on. Extend the activity to include other vowel rhymes.

Moving toys Design a large bike using strips of paper and big circles. Work together with the children to devise some safety rules for riding a bike. These can be displayed with the children's sequential instructions.

What can it be? Ask the children to sit in a circle and read out their sentences. The other children must try and guess what is inside the bag. Discuss which sentences were helpful for describing the object. Choose one or two objects and write suitable sentences to describe them. Read these sentences together pointing out that each idea forms a separate sentence that begins with a capital letter and ends with a full stop.

Can you do this? Ask the children to sit in a circle and read out their sentences in turn for a friend to carry out the instructions.

Tick-tock says the clock! Compile the children's words into groups of vowel sounds. Invite the children to choose their favourite words from the lists to create a large zig-zag book. Each page should have a separate vowel sound. Ask the children to choose one word from each page to write in to a sentence. Remind the children that each of their sentences will need to begin with a capital letter and end with a full stop.

Party invitations Talk to the children about an event that is happening at school. It might be a concert, a fête or an assembly for example. Decide with the children what essential information would be needed to display on a poster so that people would know all about it. Write their ideas on a separate piece of paper and pin it up for discussion. The children can then work in pairs to produce their posters.

Favourite fruit Make large pictures of a mouth, nose, eyes, hand and ear with the appropriate sense written alongside. Encourage the children to learn the words. Choose a different fruit each week and divide the children into five groups. Invite each group to consider a different sense. Pass the fruit around the children and write a list of words under each of the senses.

Describing fabrics Encourage the children to sort their materials using a variety of criteria, such as: smooth, rough, shiny or patterned. Ask the children to sit in a circle and place several pieces of fabric in the centre. Choose one child to describe one of the pieces while the other children turn away from the circle. When signalled, the children turn back and try to identify the fabric. If correct, this fabric is removed and the game continues.

Goldilocks Use the children's letters to make a class book. Read them out to the class. Can the childen decide which letters are apologies and which are excuses? Read *Revolting Rhymes* by Roald Dahl (Picture Puffin) or *The Jolly Postman* by Allan and Janet Ahlberg (Heinemann) to help the children to see this story from different perspectives.

Headlines Look at a selection of newspapers and the way they are set out. Make a class newspaper of the children's regular news writing.

Tea for hungry giants Do some work on size with the children. Read them the story *Jim and the Beanstalk* by Raymond Briggs (Picture Puffin). Create a display about size from the work that the children bring back in.

Please come to my party This activity draws the children's attention to reading and writing for information. Use the returned work to make a class book.

Picture dictionary Show the children some different examples of print and draw their attention to the variety of fonts and size that a letter can appear as. Ask them to find examples of a particular letter which you indicate on the sheet.

All the fun of the fair Discuss the range of words that the children have come up with. Choose some of their favourite ones to make into 'shape words'.

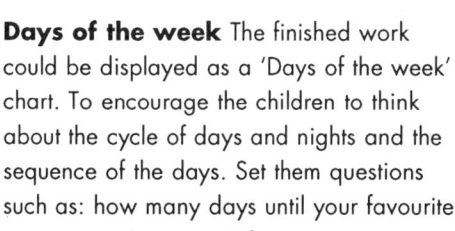

Days of the week The finished work could be displayed as a 'Days of the week' chart. To encourage the children to think about the cycle of days and nights and the sequence of the days. Set them questions such as: how many days until your favourite programme is on again?

I remember when... Display the finished work as a timeline in class. Add some fixed points to the timeline such as when the children started nursery and reception and any outings the whole class took part in.

Night work Link this activity to a topic on 'People who help us' or on work about night and day.

Alphabet furniture Make a furniture alphabet book with the ideas the children bring in. Compile lists of the furniture items in alphabetical order from the children's contributions. Display them in your writing area, with their initial letters highlighted.

Hall of fame Use the pictures to make a display or book in alphabetical order, highlighting initial letters in name labels. What other names begin with that letter? Add photographs to compare likenesses and write captions to go with the pictures about why these people are important in the lives of the children.

Holiday meals Focus on the initial letters of foods and food items highlighting them in displays of the children's drawings. Make card games of matching pairs, matching pictures and words around the theme of holiday foods. Compile a class recipe book of the children's favourite holiday foods for the children to refer to.

Short names Play a matching pair or pelanism game with the longer and shorter versions of a selection of names. Have a look at other kinds of abbreviations in names of companies, institutions or countries, for example, ITV, USA, UK and so on.

In the future Ask the children to make up a futuristic story to go with their pictures. Create a display of family albums or portraits which show the similarities and differences in family traits across generations.

Chips detective/Smart detective Make a large classroom display of a plate of chips and label each chip with a different word beginning with 'ch'. Make the display interactive by cutting the chips into two with zig-zag edges so that childen can find various endings to the initial 'ch' words. Do a similar thing with 'sm' words: cutting them into two and inviting the children to create some 'sm' words. Play a game of 'Hangman' with a 'sm' or 'ch' word or sentence.

TV stars Collect pin-ups of favourite television and movie stars from children's magazines. Arrange the labelled pin-ups in alphabetical order and display them. Ask the children to put name labels to faces or reverse the game so they have to put pin-ups to name labels.

Fantasy holiday Gather together a range of resources along the theme of holidays and travel, such as buckets and spades, train, bus and airline tickets, photographs, posters and holiday brochures. Together with the children, caption their postcards and display them with the artefacts.

Alphabet TV guide Gather the information together and make a chart of the most popular TV programmes. Play a game of TV Bingo with favourite TV programme names on the bingo cards.

Write yourself a letter! Create lots of reasons for the children to write letters and cards to each other in class to give the children practice at addressing and receiving mail. Make a classroom mailbox and address, sort and deliver internal mail. Invent some sorting postal codes for sections or zones of the classroom or even the school.

Howdy partner! Design a dictionary display of English and American words and phrases that the children bring in. Compare the spellings and look at other accents and dialects of English both from home (Devonian, Yorkshire and so on) and abroad (Australian, Jamaican, Indian and so on).

Shelf stacker Create an 'alphabet shop/supermarket': store items in alphabetical order and invite the children to write shopping lists and till receipts using initial letters.

To the helper:

- Read the rhyme together several times, pointing at each word as it is said. Look at the initial letters of the words – what does the word Humpty begin with? What other words begin with 'h'?
- Cut out each sentence separately and help your child to arrange them in the correct order.
- Help your child by giving them some clues. For example, the first two lines begin with Humpty Dumpty.

In order to read successfully your child will need to develop a good memory. Familiar rhymes and phrases help with this skill.

_____ and
child

_____
helper(s)

_____
did this activity together

Humpty Dumpty

Humpty Dumpty sat on the wall,

Humpty Dumpty had a great fall.

All the King's horses and all the King's men,

Couldn't put Humpty together again!

- Sing this song together.
- Draw a picture of Humpty Dumpty.

Writing straight letters

Most letters begin by making a line from the top to the bottom. Here are three for you to practise.

n as in nest

n

m as in monster

m

h as in hamster

h

● Write each letter four times as neatly as possible and draw a picture of something that begins with each of the letters.

To the helper:

● Before writing the letters practise by using your finger to form the letter on the paper.

● Say the writing pattern as the letter is written:
for 'n' – start at the top, down you go, up and over again;
for 'm' – start at the top, down you go, up again and over and up again and over;
for 'h' – start at the top, down you go then half way up and over.

It is essential that your child learns how to form letters properly to develop a neat legible writing style.

_____ and
child

_____
helper(s)

_____
did this activity together

To the helper:

- Please encourage your child to use their finger on the paper to make a nice curly shape like a 'c'.
- When your child is confident with this shape hold their hand while you make the 'a' shape together. As you write, say – curl round the c and join it up, now straight down to make 'a'.
- Encourage your child to write in the air with their finger and use felt-tipped pens to make patterns with the letters.

In order for children to be able to write quickly and legibly it is important to form letters correctly from the beginning.

_____ and

child

_____

helper(s)

_____

did this activity together

Curly letters

All these letters belong to the curly cat writing family.

This letter makes the 'c' sound you hear at the beginning of cat.
Try not to let your pencil lift off the paper until the letter is finished.

This letter makes the 'a' sound you hear at the beginning of ant, apple, alligator and ambulance.

This letter makes the 'd' sound you hear at the beginning of donkey, duck, dragon and dinosaur.

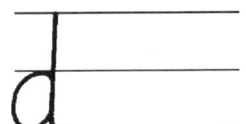

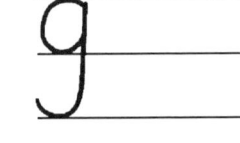

This letter makes the 'g' sound you hear at the beginning of garden, gate and garage.

- Write each letter and draw a picture to go with it.

Early years activities

impact WRITING HOMEWORK

Doing words

- Draw four pictures that show something happening.

- Choose one of your pictures and tell your helper what is happening. Ask them to write down what you have said for you to copy underneath. For example – I am swinging on a swing in the garden.

To the helper:

- Talk about your child's pictures with them.
- Encourage them to describe their doing words, for example: I am running very quickly to catch the bus.

Children enjoy describing their activities. In order to be successful speakers and then writers they need to be able to extend their ideas to make them more interesting.

_____ and
child

_____
helper(s)

_____
did this activity together

Early years activities

To the helper:

- Children love hearing rhymes and rhythms. Help them to make sentences that contain many repeating sounds.
- It often helps to write a list of words before trying to compose a sentence.

Many children find reading much easier if there is a rhyme or rhythm to the text. Reading poems and rhymes together is an excellent way of encouraging children to read and remember words. This activity also reinforces letter sound recognition.

_____ and
child

_____
helper(s)

_____
did this activity together

64   Early years activities

Alliteration

What sound does the first letter of your name make?

- Think of some other words that start with the same letter. Now try and put them all together to make a funny sentence like these ones:

Emma enjoys enormous Easter eggs!

Shareen shouts at the sharks near the ship!

- Now write a sensational sentence for everyone in your house. Choose your favourite one and draw a picture to go with it.

impact WRITING HOMEWORK

Shopping list

- Help your family by writing down five or six things you need from the supermarket.

- Ask if you can copy the names from the packets or labels of things in the fridge or in the cupboard.

To the helper:

- Your child may be able to suggest what is needed on the list.
- Encourage your child to listen to the first sound in the word to help them try to write it. For example 'c' in custard.
- Perhaps your child could write the beginning letters before you write the remaining letters.
- Try to find the words on labels in the supermarket and on the till receipts.

It is important for children to realise that reading is everywhere – not just in their reading books. It helps them to believe in themselves as readers.

_____and
child

_____
helper(s)

_____

did this activity together

Early years activities

To the helper:

- Help your child by going through the alphabet adding letters to the 'at' sound. For example, make the sound 'b' and add it to make 'bat'.
- Read the words together.
- Help your child to compose a silly sentence, please be the scribe if this is appropriate.

Hearing rhythms and rhymes in words is essential for reading and writing skills.

The 'at' family

How many words can you write that rhyme with 'at'?

- Make a list and use some of them to make a silly sentence!
- Draw a picture to go with your sentence.

_____and
child

_____
helper(s)

_____
did this activity together

Early years activities

Moving toys

- Draw a bike or a moving toy here.

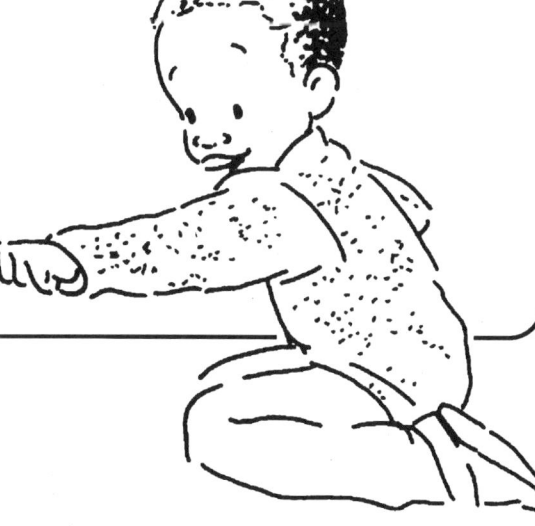

How do you make your bike or toy travel?

- Think about what you do and try to say what you do in the correct order.

To the helper:

- Encourage your child to be precise about what happens in sequence.
- Write the instructions on separate pieces of paper for your child.
- Read the instructions together and stick them in the agreed order.
- Ask your child to check that nothing has been forgotten by riding their bicycle or moving their toy.

Writing instructions is a difficult skill to master and requires a lot of practice. It involves writing short 'bossy' sentences, for example: 'hold the handlebars'.

_____and

child

_____

helper(s)

_____

did this activity together

impact WRITING HOMEWORK

Early years activities

To the helper:

- Talk about your child's chosen toy with them. Encourage them to describe the essential characteristics of their toy.
- Write down their suggestions for them.
- Read them together and decide which three descriptions are the most appropriate.

In order for children to use language effectively they will need to develop a wide vocabulary. This activity will help children to learn how to describe accurately.

_____and

child

_____

helper(s)

_____

did this activity together

68 Early years activities

What can it be?

- Choose a small toy and write three sentences to describe it.

- Take your toy into school – hide it in a bag and don't let anyone see it!

- Read out your sentences to the class, don't say what it is and see if they can guess.

impact WRITING HOMEWORK

Can you do this?

- Stand on one leg.
  Bounce up and down.
  Keep balanced as you bounce.

Can you describe what you are doing?

- Describe another movement to your helper.
Is your helper able to follow your instructions?

To the helper:

- Help your child to describe what is happening in the correct order.
- Write down the instructions on separate pieces of paper. Read them together and decide if the instructions and order are right.

Being able to describe instructions is very difficult and is an important writing skill. This will give your child practice of sequencing events accurately, which will help when they are writing stories.

_____ and
child

_____
helper(s)

_____

did this activity together

To the helper:

- Concentrate on one vowel sound at a time. For example just 'ock' words to begin with. If your child finds it difficult to hear the different vowel sounds then concentrate on one or two of them.
- Try to remember to use the vowel sound, as in 'o' for otter and not the vowel name as in 'o' for open.

Children love learning rhyming words. The vowel sounds in the middle of words are difficult for young children to hear and they need plenty of opportunities to learn about them.

_____and
child

_____
helper(s)

_____
did this activity together

70 **Early years activities**

Tick-tock says the clock!

Can you hear the 'curly c' and 'kicking k' sound at the end of tick, tock and clock?

● Think of some letters that fill these gaps to make a word:

_____ock   _____ick

_____ack   _____uck

● Draw a picture to go with your favourite 'ck' word.

impact WRITING HOMEWORK

Party invitations

- Pretend you are having a party.
You will need to write some invitations.

What do you need to put on your invitations?
Will your party have a theme?
How will you decorate your invitation?

- Write your invitation here.

To the helper:

- Have a look at some invitations in your local shop to give you some ideas.
- Help your child to decide what they would like to say and write the information for them if necessary.
- Read the details together pointing out each word. Your child can then copy the invitation in the space.

This activity will help your child to focus on essential information. It will give their writing a sense of purpose.

_____and
child

_____
helper(s)

_____

did this activity together

To the helper:
- Please help your child to write their ideas. It may help them to focus on one of the senses at a time.
- Ask your child to copy their favourite ideas into the spaces. Read them through together afterwards.
- Try out the descriptions on someone else in your home. Can they guess which fruit is your child's favourite from their descriptions?

This activity will give the children an opportunity to develop a vocabulary of words to describe their senses.

_____ and
child

_____
helper(s)

_____
did this activity together

Favourite fruit

- Describe your favourite fruit using two of your five senses.

- Do not name your fruit, keep it hidden until you have read out your descriptions.

- Draw a picture of it.

72 **Early years activities**

impact WRITING HOMEWORK

Describing fabrics

- Ask at home for a small piece of patterned fabric.
- Describe the colour, pattern and feel of your fabric.

Is the fabric thick or thin?
What could it be used for?
Why do you think this?

To the helper:

- Help your child to look carefully at the fabric. Draw their attention to the features of the fabric by asking: what colours are in the fabric? Is there a repeating pattern? Does it feel soft and silky or hard and shiny? Is the fabric thick or thin?
- Help your child to imagine what the fabric might be used for.

It is important to be able to describe several characteristics about an item. This encourages children to be descriptive and imaginative about their observations.

_____and
child

_____
helper(s)

_____

did this activity together

Early years activities

To the helper:

- Read the story of Goldilocks together, or retell it from memory.
- Discuss why Goldilocks will need to apologise. What will she say? Will she say she is naughty or will she make excuses? What could her excuses be? Will she try to make amends?
- After your child has discussed their ideas with you help them to write down what they want to say.

Thinking of imaginative ideas is very important and your child will need to develop this by discussing ideas with you.

_____ and
child

_____
helper(s)

did this activity together

74 **Early years activities**

Goldilocks

- Imagine that you are Goldilocks and the three bears have asked you to apologise for your behaviour in their cottage.

- Write a letter saying you are sorry.

impact WRITING HOMEWORK

Headlines

- Draw and write about an event that has happened to you.

To the helper:

- Talk about things that have happened to your child. Encourage them to decide which things are 'newsworthy'.
- Look at some newspaper headlines together and talk about how they are written.
- Encourage your child to choose an event and write about it in the style of a newspaper headline. For example: Sabrina's tooth finally falls out!

This activity introduces children to a different style of writing.

_____and
child

_____
helper(s)

_____

did this activity together

Early years activities

To the helper:

- Encourage your child to use their imagination and talk about the large amounts of food that will be needed.
- Make it fun and use as much descriptive language as possible. For example: they will need a jelly as big as a pond!
- Use large numbers as well!

This activity helps develop the children's imagination and descriptive powers. It combines informative and imaginative writing.

_____ and
child

_____
helper(s)

did this activity together

Tea for hungry giants!

● Write a shopping list for a giants' tea party.

Remember giants have enormous appetites!

76 **Early years activities**

impact WRITING HOMEWORK

Please come to my party

- Imagine it is your birthday and you can invite anyone you like to your birthday party. Who would you like to ask?

- Write a letter to someone famous asking them to come to your birthday party.

To the helper:

- Talk about your child's choice of person. Why do they like that person?
- Help them to decide what information needs to be included in the letter such as the date, time and place. They could also tell their chosen person why they are special to them.

This activity gives the child a purpose for writing and helps them to learn about certain writing conventions. It also encourages imaginative writing in a meaningful way.

_____and
child

_____
helper(s)

_____

did this activity together

To the helper:

- Help your child to use catalogues, magazines, advertisements and newspapers to find as many things beginning with their letter as they can.

Back in class we will look at each other's pictures and then use them to create a class dictionary. This activity will also help children to learn the sequence of the letters of the alphabet.

_____ and

child

_____

helper(s)

_____

did this activity together

78   Early years activities

Picture dictionary

Your letter is _____.

- Collect some pictures of things beginning with this letter.

impact WRITING HOMEWORK

All the fun of the fair

Have you ever been to the fair or seen some pictures of one?

- Think of as many words as you can about fairgrounds. Make a list of them.

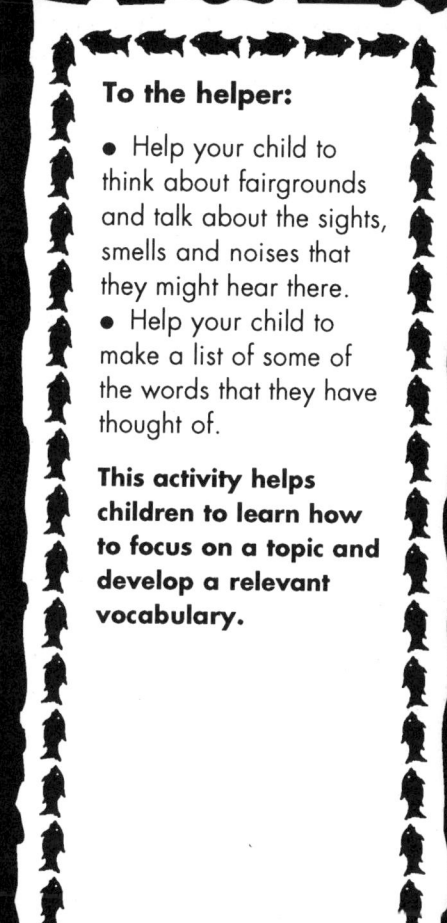

To the helper:

- Help your child to think about fairgrounds and talk about the sights, smells and noises that they might hear there.
- Help your child to make a list of some of the words that they have thought of.

This activity helps children to learn how to focus on a topic and develop a relevant vocabulary.

_____ and
child

_____
helper(s)

_____

did this activity together

To the helper:

- Help your child to find the information they need. Use a TV guide or the newspaper and show your child how to find what they are looking for.
- Discuss with your child how many times a week the programme is on: is it on at the same time each week or day?

This activity will help build up your child's knowledge of the days of the week. It will also give them an insight into how we use reference materials to find out information.

_____ and
child

_____
helper(s)

_____
did this activity together

80   **Early years activities**

Days of the week

What is your favourite TV programme?

- Find out what day of the week it is on and write it down, along with the time it is on.

impact WRITING HOMEWORK

I remember when...

Can you remember the things you used to do when you were very little?

- Draw and write about your earliest memory.

To the helper:

- Discuss with your child some of the things they did when they were little. Try to encourage your child to think back as far as they can.
- When your child has decided on an event such as an outing or a party, talk about how old they were at the time. Try to use words that describe the past such as, a long time ago or when I was little.

This activity helps to increase children's awareness of the past. It helps them to develop a basic historical vocabulary.

_____ and
child

_____
helper(s)

_____
did this activity together

To the helper:

- Help your child to think of some jobs that people do during the night.
Begin by thinking about places that need to stay open such as hospitals and police stations.
- Help your child to think of a job that they would like to do.

This activity encourages children to think about the day/night cycle in an imaginative way. It also increases their awareness of lifestyles other than their own.

_____and

child

_____

helper(s)

_____

did this activity together

Early years activities

Night work

Some people have jobs that mean they have to work during the night. Can you think of a job that you would like to do at night?

- Draw a picture and write something about the job.

impact WRITING HOMEWORK

Alphabet furniture

How many letters of the alphabet do you know that begin the name of a piece of furniture, ornament or household object in your house?

● When you think of an object ask your helper to write down the name of the piece of furniture. Learn the name of the first letter and colour it in.

To the helper:

● Talk about the first letters of furniture names and help your child find the letter in the alphabet.
● As you write the name of the piece of furniture focus on the first letter and help your child learn its name.
● Write out the letters and words slowly so your child can see how the shapes of the letters are formed.
● Let your child have a go at forming the letters. Don't worry if you can't find 26 things!

This activity helps children learn the letters of the alphabet in a context that uses their own knowledge.

_____and
child

_____
helper(s)

_____

did this activity together

Early years activities

To the helper:

- Discuss with your child who their favourite people are and why they like them more than anyone else. This will help them to put their thoughts in order.
- Write out the letters and names slowly so your child can see how the shapes of the letters are formed.
- Spell out the names so your child will begin to learn the letters.

This activity introduces children to writing lists and using writing to order their thoughts and priorities.

_____ and
child

_____
helper(s)

did this activity together

Hall of fame

Who are your favourite people?

- Draw a picture of your five favourite people and write their names underneath.

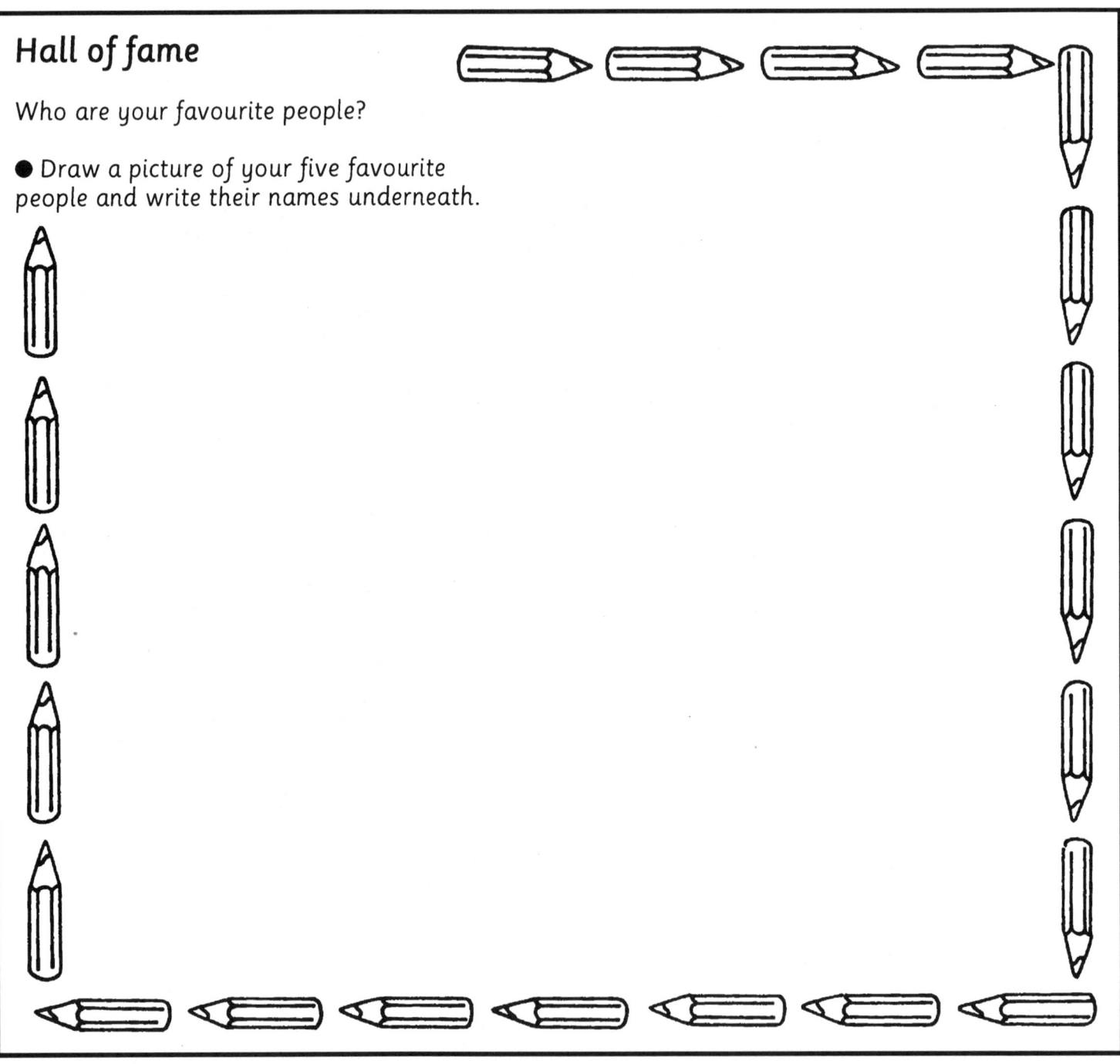

Holiday meals

Which is your favourite holiday meal?
Do you like picnics, barbeques or TV suppers?

● Draw a picture of your favourite holiday meal and label all the ingredients.

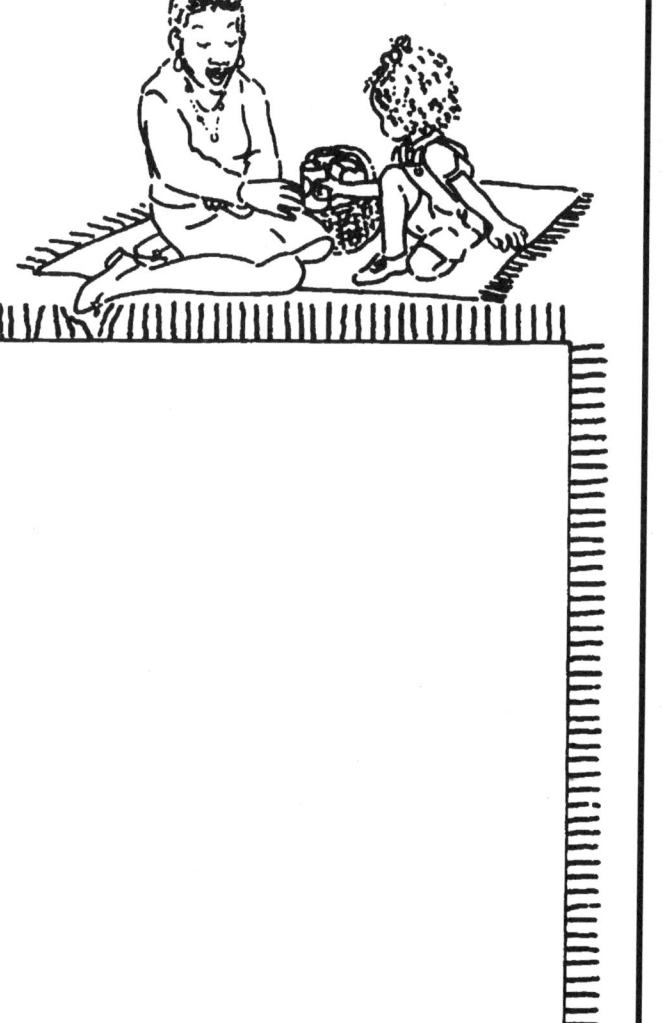

To the helper:

● Talk about the meals you have on outings, holidays or special occasions.

● Help with the spellings and writing in the labels for the picture. Write out letters and words slowly so your child can see how the shapes of the letters are formed. Then let them have a go.

This activity helps children to understand the conventions of labelling and gives a purpose to their writing.

_____and
child

_____
helper(s)

_____
did this activity together

To the helper:

- Write down the long and short version of names so your child can see how the shorter name (usually) comes from the longer one.
- Write out letters and words slowly, drawing attention to the way you form the letters. Spell out the names so your child will begin to learn the letters.

This activity introduces the concept of abbreviation in a context that is familiar and meaningful to them.

_____and
child
_____
helper(s)
_____
did this activity together

Short names

Ben is short for Benjamin, Pat is short for Patricia, Dev is short for Hardev.

How many shortened names can you think of from family, relatives, friends or neighbours?

● Write down as many as you can think of.

86 Early years activities

impact WRITING HOMEWORK

In the future

What do you think you will look like in five, ten, thirty and sixty years time?

What clothes will you be wearing? What will your hair-style be like?

- Draw four pictures of yourself in the future. Write a caption for each picture.

To the helper:

- Talk about possible clothes fashions, hair-styles and lifestyles of the future and have some fun imagining what your child will look like.
- Talk about the ageing process and what effect it will have on their physical appearance. Discuss family likeness across generations and if possible look at some old photos.
- Help your child with the writing.

This activity will help children develop ideas about the future which they will be able to use in their writing.

_____and
child

_____
helper(s)

_____
did this activity together

Early years activities

To the helper:

- Simply brainstorm all the words that you can both think of for words with the same beginning sound (for example, chase, chance and cheap).
- Do the same for the ending sound (for example, hips and lips).

This activity helps children become more aware of ending as well as beginning sounds in words as they learn to read and write. This will help with the development of their reading and writing skills.

_____ and

child

_____

helper(s)

did this activity together

Early years activities

Chips detective

How many things can you think of that begin with the same sound as **ch**ips?

How many things can you think of that end with the same sound as ch**ips**?

- With your helper, make a list of the ones that you thought of.

impact WRITING HOMEWORK

Smart detective

How many words can you think of that begin with the same sound as **sm**art?

How many words can you think of that end with the same sound as sm**art**?

- With your helper, make a list of the ones that you thought of.

To the helper:

- Simply brainstorm all the words that you can both think of with the same beginning sound (for example small, smashing and smelly).
- Do the same with the ending sound (for example, dart, heart and cart).

This activity helps children become more aware of ending as well as beginning sounds. This will help with the development of their reading and writing skills.

_____ and
child

_____
helper(s)

_____
did this activity together

To the helper:

- Discuss with your child who their favourite TV stars are and why.
- Help them to spell out their names and write them underneath their pictures. It may be best to do this in rough first and copy it neatly on to the paper afterwards. As you help them to write the names draw their attention to the use of a capital letter to begin a person's name.

This activity introduces children to the use of capital letters for people's names and gives them valuable writing and spelling practice.

_____ and
child

_____
helper(s)

_____
did this activity together

90 **Early years activities**

TV stars

Who are your favourite TV stars?

- Draw their faces here and write their names underneath.

impact WRITING HOMEWORK

Fantasy holiday

- Draw a picture of yourself on the best holiday you can imagine.

- Cut out your drawing, paste it to a card or envelope and send yourself the postcard.

To the helper:

- Talk to your child about a fantasy holiday that they would love to go on. Encourage them to think of the things that they would do there, the people they would meet and the places they would visit.
- Help them to write their greeting and their address and send it off in the post.

This activity helps children to use their imagination to write. It also helps them to see the practical purpose of sending greetings cards.

_____ and
child

_____
helper(s)

_____
did this activity together

Early years activities

To the helper:

- It might help your child if you write out the alphabet first.
- Talk about the first letters in the TV programmes and help your child to find the letter in the alphabet.
- Help your child to write their list, focusing on the first letter and helping your child to learn its name.

This activity gives the children practice in learning the names and sounds of the letters in the alphabet.

_____ and
child

_____
helper(s)

_____
did this activity together

92 **Early years activities**

Alphabet TV guide

Think of your favourite TV programmes. What letters do they begin with?

● Make a list of them. Draw a circle around the first letter of their names. Are they all different or are some of them the same?

impact WRITING HOMEWORK

Write yourself a letter!

- Learn your address and how to write it.
- Fill in this label, cut it out, stick it to an envelope or card and send it to yourself!
- Don't forget to write yourself a greeting!

To the helper:

- Make sure your child can recite their own address and then help them learn to write it. You may need to help them with letters and words.
- Post some letters from different post boxes. Do they arrive at the same time. Investigate how long it takes for First and Second Class letters to arrive.

This activity helps children learn that writing can have practical purposes and it will help them learn to write their names and addresses.

_____ and
child

_____
helper(s)

_____

did this activity together

impact WRITING HOMEWORK

Early years activities

To the helper:

- Talk about American films and TV programmes that you watch and the differences in accent (pronunciation) and vocabulary (words).
- Help your child to find out the American equivalents of the words on the page.

This activity demonstrates that English is an international language and that variations of vocabulary are in use in the different countries where it is spoken.

_____and
child

_____
helper(s)

did this activity together

94   **Early years activities**

Howdy partner!

Do you know any 'American-English' words and phrases?

● Draw some speech bubbles with American phrases.

Do you know any others?

What do Americans call:

a lift _____

a film _____

a lorry _____

lemonade _____

a pavement _____

beefburger and chips _____

impact WRITING HOMEWORK

Shelf stacker

- Help your helper to pack away all the items that have been bought from a grocery shopping trip.

- Use the till receipt to make sure every item is accounted for and show this by putting a tick next to each item.

Can you find one item for each letter of the alphabet?

A _____
B _____
C _____
D _____
E _____
F _____
G _____
H _____
I _____
J _____
K _____
L _____
M _____

N _____
O _____
P _____
Q _____
R _____
S _____
T _____
U _____
V _____
W _____
X _____
Y _____
Z _____

To the helper:

- As you unpack each item of shopping, look at it carefully, examine the label and together make the sound of the first letter.
- Find the letter on the till receipt and help your child to decipher some of the words. What other letters do they recognise?
- Look at the alphabet and find an item for as many letters as you can.
- Write out letters and words slowly so your child can see how the shapes of the letters are formed.

This activity helps children learn about letter names and their sounds in a familiar context.

_____ and
child

_____
helper(s)

_____

did this activity together

Early years activities

IMPACT schools

We are trying to compile a list of IMPACT schools so that we can:
- inform you as new materials are produced;
- offer help and support via our INSET office;
- find out the spread of this type of shared writing homework.

Also, because it is helpful if you have support and advice when starting up a shared homework scheme, we have a team of registered in-service trainers around Britain. Through the IMPACT office we can arrange for whole day, half day or 'twilight' sessions in schools.

I would like further information about IMPACT INSET sessions.

YES/NO

Please photocopy and cut off this strip and return it to:

The IMPACT Office,
Education Dept.,
University of North London,
Holloway Road,
London N7 8DB.
0171 753 7052

Teacher's name _____

School's name _____

Address _____

LEA _____

Management

Most teachers send the shared writing task as a photocopied sheet included in the children's **Reading Folder** or in their IMPACT **Maths folder**. Remind the children that they may use the back of the IMPACT sheet to write on. Before the activity is sent home, it is crucial that the teacher prepares the children for the task. This may involve reading a story, going over some ideas or having a group or class discussion. Some ideas are provided here in the Teachers' Notes for each activity. The importance of this preparation cannot be overstressed.

Many of the tasks done at home lend themselves naturally to a display or enable the teacher to make a class-book. A shared writing display board in the entrance hall of the school gives parents an important sense that their work at home is appreciated and valued.

The shared writing activity sheets can be stuck into an exercise book kept specifically for this purpose. Any follow-up work that the children do in school can also be put into this book. As the books go back and forth with the activity sheets this enables parents to see how the work at home has linked to work in class.

Non-IMPACTers

We know that parental support is a key factor in children's education and children who cannot find anyone with whom to share the writing task may be losing out. Try these strategies:
- Encourage, cajole and reward the children who bring back their shared writing. If a child – and parent/carer – does the task haphazardly, praise the child whenever the task is completed, rather than criticise if it does not.
- If possible, invite a couple of parents in to share the activities with the children. This involves parents in the life of the school as well as making sure that some children don't lose out.
- Some schools set up 'writing partners' between children in two different classes pairing a child from Y6 with a child in Y1 for shared writing activities, perhaps weekly or fortnightly.

None of these strategies is perfect, but many parents will help when they can and with encouragement, will join in over the longer term.

Useful information and addresses

The IMPACT shared maths scheme is running successfully in thousands of schools in the UK and abroad. The shared writing works in the same way, and obviously complements the maths very well. Both fit in with the shared reading initiatives (PACT or CAPER) which many schools also run. The OFSTED Inspection Schedules require and take account of schools working with parents as well as the quality of teaching and learning. IMPACT receives positive mentions in inspectors' reports.

Further information from: The IMPACT Project, School of Teaching Studies, University of North London, 166–220 Holloway Road, London N7 8DB.

The Shared Maths Homework books can be obtained from Scholastic Ltd, Westfield Road, Southam, Warwickshire CV33 0JH.

For IMPACT Diaries contact: IMPACT Supplies, PO Box 126, Witney, Oxfordshire OX8 5YL. Tel: 01993 774408.

Curricula links

Activities in this book support the Language and Literacy area of SCAA's Desirable Outcomes for Children's Learning. In addition the following requirements are also met.

National Curriculum: English, KS1 Writing
1. Range – a,b,c
2. Key Skills – a, b, c, d, e
3. Standard English and Language Study – a,b

Scottish 5-14 Guidelines: English Language	
Strand	Level
Functional writing	A
Punctuation and structure	A/B
Spelling	A
Handwriting and presentation	A/B
Knowledge about language	B

Northern Ireland Curriculum: English
Within meaningful contexts, pupils should be taught:
• to write and know the names of a variety of forms;
• to form letter shapes in upper and lower case;
• the names and order of the letters of the alphabet;
• to write correctly structured sentences.